JAPAN

Understanding & Dealing With The New Japanese Way Of Doing Business!

***

In 1853 the U.S. send a fleet of warships to Japan to force the Shogun and the ruling samurai class to initiate diplomatic and trade relations with the outside world.
The record-keeper of Commodore Perry's fleet added the following footnote to his log:

"The Japanese will surprise the World!"

***

THE FOUNDATIONS OF JAPANESE BEHAVIOR

JAPAN

Understanding & Dealing With The New Japanese Way Of Doing Business!

Boyé Lafayette De Mente

A PHOENIX BOOKS ORIGINAL

Copyright © 2012 by Boyé Lafayette De Mente
All rights reserved

Other Books by the Author

[Books on China]
The Chinese Mind—Understanding Traditional Chinese Beliefs and their Influence on Contemporary Culture
CHINA—Understanding and Dealing with the Chinese Way of Doing Business
China's Cultural Code Words [Key Chinese Terms that Reveal the Culture and Mindset of the Chinese]
Chinese in Plain English
Survival Chinese
Instant Chinese
Etiquette Guide to China—Know the Rules that Make the Difference

[Books on Japan]
KATA—The Key to Understanding & Dealing with the Japanese
Japan's Cultural Code Words
Exotic Japan—The Sensual & Visual Pleasures
Discovering Cultural Japan
Speak Japanese Today—A Little Language Goes a Long Way!
Instant Japanese
Survival Japanese
Japan Made Easy—All You Need to Know to Enjoy Japan
Etiquette Guide to Japan—Know the Rules that Make the Difference
The Japanese Samurai Code—Classic Strategies for Success
Japan Unmasked—The Character & Culture of the Japanese
Elements of Japanese Design—Understanding & Using Japan's Classic *Wabi-Sabi-Shibui* Concepts
Samurai Strategies—42 Secret Martial Arts from Musashi's "Book of Five Rings"
Why the Japanese are a Superior People—The Advantages of Using Both Sides of Your Brain!
Amazing Japan—Why Japan is one of the World's Most Intriguing Countries

THE FOUNDATIONS OF JAPANESE BEHAVIOR

Exotic Japan—The Sensual & Visual Pleasures
SABURO—The Saga of a Teenage Samurai in 17th Century Japan
The Bizarre & the Wondrous from the Land of the Rising Sun!

[Books on Korea]
THE KOREAN MIND—Understanding & Dealing with Koreans
Korean Business Etiquette
Korean in Plain English
Etiquette Guide to Korea—Know the Rules that Make the Difference
Instant Korean
Survival Korean

[Books on Mexico]
Why Mexicans Think & Behave the Way They Do—The Cultural Factors that Created the Character & Personality of the Mexican People
THE MEXICAN MIND – Understanding & Appreciating Mexican Culture
ROMANTIC MEXICO—The Image & the Realities

[Other Titles]
Which Side of Your Brain Am I Talking To? – The Advantages of Using Both Sides of Your Brain
Samurai Principles & Practices that will Help Preteens & Teens in School, Sports, Social Activities & Choosing Careers
Romantic Hawaii – Sun, Sand, Surf & Sex
Asian Face Reading – Unlock the Secrets Hidden in the Human Face
Bridging Cultural Barriers in China, Japan, Korea & Mexico
Brave New World of American Sex!
THE WOMAN IN THE BLUE BRA! – A Message to the World!
ONCE A FOOL – From Japan to Alaska by Amphibious Jeep!

CONTENTS

INTRODUCTION

The Rise & Fall of Japan As the World's 2nd Largest Economic Superpower

PART 1

The Changing Face Of Japanese Business

PART 2

The Foundations of Japan's Business Culture

Wa [Wah] / The Foundation of Japanese Behavior
Amae [Ah-my] / The Building Blocks of Wa
Kata [kah-tah] / The Role of Form in Japanese Behavior
Makoto [Mah-koe-toe] / Sincerity, Japanese Style
Shinyo [Sheen-yoh] / Trusting the Way of Wa
Uramu [Uu-rah-muu] / That Hostile Feeling
Enryo [In-ree-oh] / Holding Back
Giseisha [Ghee-say-e-shah] / The Victim Syndrome
Chokkan to Roni [Choke-kahn toh Roan-ree] / Intuition plus. Logic
Shudan Ishiki [Shuu-dahn Ee-she-kee] / All Together Now

THE FOUNDATIONS OF JAPANESE BEHAVIOR

On [Own] / The Web that Binds
Giri [Ghee-ree] / The Personal Code
Ninjo [Neen-joe] / Human Feelings Come First
Chishiki [Chee-she-kee] / The Japanese Way of Perceiving and Using Knowledge
Koto to Shidai ni Wa [Koh-to to She-die nee Wah] / Circumstantial Truth
Jicho [Jee-choh] / Staying out of Trouble
Kao wo Tateru [Kow oh Tah-tay-rue] / Save My Face
Tatemae/Honne [Tah-tay-my/Hone-nay] / The Two-Faced Syndrome
Oyabun / Kobun [Oh-yah-boon / Koe-boon] / Living and Working in a Vertical Society
Tsukiai [T'sue-kee-aye] / Paying Social Debts
Kaisha [Kie-shah] / The Company as a Community
Ichi-ryu, Ni-ryu, San-ryu / [Ee-chee-re-yuu, Nee-re-yu, Sahn-re-yuu] First-class, Second-class, Third-class
Shikomu [She-koe-muu] / Training in Company Morality
Shakai no Kurabu [Shah-kie no Kuu-rah-buu] / The Company as a Social Club
Juyaka [Juu-yah-kuu] / Top Executives
Ka [Kah] / People in Boxes
Bu [Buu] / Finding the Right Department
Shu-Shin Koyo [Shuu-Sheen Koh-yoh] / Lifetime Employment
Nenko Joretsu [Nane-koe Joe-rate-sue] / The Merit of Years
Sabisu [Sah-bee-sue] / The Japanese Version of Service
Jimusho no Hana [Jeem-show no Hah-nah] / "Office Flowers"
Rinji Saiyo [Reen-jee Sie-yoe] / The Outsiders

THE FOUNDATIONS OF JAPANESE BEHAVIOR

Seishin [Say-e-sheen] / Training the Spirit
Onjo Shugi [Own-joe Shuu-ghee] / "Mothering" Employees
Risshin Shusse [Rees-sheen Shuus-say] / The Japanese Success Drive
Katagaki [Kah-tah-gah-kee] / The Importance of Rank
Sempai – Kohai [Sim-pie Koh-hi] / Seniors and Juniors
Kaizen [Kie-zen] / The Continuous Improvement Concept
Gyosei Shido [G'yoh-say-ee She-doh] / Government Guidance
Amakudari [Ah-mah-kuu-dah-ree] / Descending from Heaven
Meishi [May-e-she] / Presenting Your Face
Ojigi [Oh-jee-ghee] / Politeness Makes Perfect
Habatsu [Hah-baht-sue] / Behavior by the Numbers
Gakubatsu [Gah-kuu-baht-sue] / Rule by Cliques
Nenbatsu [Nane-baht-sue] / Up by the Year
Shokaijo [Show-kie-joe] / The All-Important Introductions
Hoshonin [Hoe-show-neen] / The Important Role of Guarantors
Chukai-Sha [Chuu-kie-Shah] / The Essential Go-Between
Kyoso [K'yoh-soh] / Competition by the Numbers
Ringi Seido [Reen-ghee Say-ee-doe] / Putting It in Writing
Nemawashi [Nay-mah-wah-she] / Behind the Scenes Lobbying
Kaigi [Kie-ghee] / Meeting to Talk
Hishokan [He-show-kahn] / Where are all the Secretaries?
Keiyaku [Kay-e-yah-kuu] / The Japanese Contract
Sekinin Sha [Say-kee-neen Shah] / Finding Where the Buck Stops
O'Miyage [Oh-Me-yah-gay] / Giving to the Cause

THE FOUNDATIONS OF JAPANESE BEHAVIOR

Moshiwake Arimasen [Moe-she-wah-kay Ah-ree-mah-sin] / Apology without End
Inseki Jinin [Een-say-kee Jee-neen] / The Japanese Cop-Out
Mizu Shobai [Me-zoo Show-by] / The "Water Business"
Bo Nen Kai [Boh Nane Kie] / Meeting to Forget
Rikutsu-poi [Ree-kute-sue-poy] / Beware of being too Logical
Wa/Sa [Wah / Sah] / Harmony vs. I'd Rather not Say
Shokaijo [Show-kie-joe] / A Shortcut to Success
O'Machigae [O'Mah-chee-guy] / A Mistake Westerners Make
San [Sahn] / The San Conundrum
Dekoboko [Deh-koe-boe-koe] / Doing Business on a Tilted Field
Mono-no-Aware [Moe-no no Ah-wah-ray] / Aesthetics in Business

PART 3

Matome
[Mah-toe-may]
Summing Up
Business-Related Websites

PART 4

Other Key Terms In Japan's Business Vocabulary

THE FOUNDATIONS OF JAPANESE BEHAVIOR

Chokkan / Ronri
[Choke-kahn / Roan-ree]
Intuition / Logic

The Japanese Advantage of Using
Both Sides of Their Brains!

INTRODUCTION

The Rise & Fall of Japan As the World's 2nd Largest Economic Superpower

How Japan is Reinventing Itself

The rise of Japan as an economic superpower between 1948 and 1970, following a disastrous defeat in World War II, was one of the most surprising and astounding events of the 20th century. But there was a precedent for this amazing accomplishment that was either unknown or had been forgotten by virtually all Americans and other Westerners—a precedent initiated in 1853 by the United States.

In that year the United States sent a fleet of warships under the command of Commodore Matthew C. Perry to Japan to force the ruling Shogunate government to open its doors to trade and diplomatic relations with the the outside world—doors that had been closed since 1637.

At that time Japan's agricultural and shopkeeper economy had changed very litle for close to a thousand years. But the traditional social culture of the country was sophisticated to an extraordinary degree, and the Japanese had a fund of technical knowledge and expertise that went back to ancient times and was to play a leading role in the future of the country and the world.

The arrival of Perry prompted a rebellion by provincial lords in the southwestern part of the country that brought about the the downfall of the Shogunate system of government in 1867. The rebels established a new parliamentary government, brought in several thousand experts from the United States, Great Britain and Germany, and began a crash program to industrialize the economy.

Between 1870 and 1895—in an astounding demonstration of energy and skill—Japan became a major industrial and military power that was to have a profound influence on the rest of the world. Like the Romans of old the newly transformed Japanese began military and economic campaigns that were to make them the overlords of Korea, Manchuria, much of China and Southeast Asia, and a serious threat to the Pacific interests of the United States.

The Japanese military threat to the U.S. ended with the defeat of Japan in the summer of 1945, and by 1960 the Japanese had not only recovered from the devastating destruction of the war they had mounted an economic invasion of the United States that appeared to be on the verge of colonizing the whole country.

The story of this economic invasion and the cultural factors that gave Japanese companies such an advantage over their American counterparts is one of the great sagas of success and failure in modern times—the success of the traditional Japanese way of doing business and the failure of the American way.

By the mid-1960s Japan had vaulted ahead of the United States and most other countries in using the latest technology in building and sustaining its transportation infrastructure. Its first "bullet train" went into operation in 1964. Its commutor transportation system became the best in the world in the 1970s. The trains and subways departed and arrived on time. This efficiency resulted in the most common refrain one heard from visitors and foreign residents alike being: "In Japan things work!"

By the early 1970s Japan was the second largest economy in the world. By the end of the 1980s the Japanese were also well ahead of the United States and other countries in applying electronic technology to a variety of commercial uses, including cell phones and text messaging.

However, in the 1970s Japan's financial and real estate industries began adopting American practices—a move that was to result in a financial melt-down that began in the mid-1980s and came to a head in the early 1990s.

Tsuyoshi Sunohara, director of the Office of Global Studies at the Japan Center for Economic Research, says that another reason for the financial and economic melt-downs that hit Japan in the 1980s and early 1990s resulted in part from an isolationist streak in the Japanese character coupled with the belief that they could lead a rich and secure life for the foreseeable future without making dramatic changes in their attitudes and behavior.

Also by the 1980s the Japanese had begun to encounter competition from South Korea, Taiwan, Hong Kong and a resurgent United States that clashed with their traditional management practices, forcing them to begin adopting a number of American business practices in a desperate effort to put their companies are more of an equal footing with these powerful competitors. Then in the 1990s a newly transformed China began to take over Japan's role as the primary producer of consumer goods for world markets.

Another key factor in the ongoing transition from purely Japanese style management to a hybrid Japanese-Western style was that Japan's home markets were saturated and their only growth potential was in foreign markets. These market forces were rapidly changing Japan from a fully *monozukuri* [moe-no-zoo-kuu-ree] or "make things" economy to one that emphasized the creation of new technology, new materials and software.

A key part of these changes was a massive outsourcing movement, first into China and then into Southeast Asian countries and India—an example first set by the United States shortly after the downfall of the feudal Tokugawa Shogunate government in 1867, when large numbers of American businesses began outsourcing their production to Japan.

In late 1989 eminent historian Minoru Nakamura said that for Japan the era of constantly rising GNP was over and that the only sensible recourse was to emphasize maturity [the quality of life] over growth.

By the mid-1990s systematic failures in the traditional aspects of Japanese management in business and politics, coupled with the rapid rise of China and other Asian countries, had reached a tipping point. These problems were exacerbated by an aging and diminishing population and by a loss of the gung-ho attitude of younger Japanese who had never known poverty or travail.

Japan's international corporations began to appeal to universities to train their students to think and behave outside of the parameters of the traditional culture—to think and behave independently and to adopt a global perspective. Some of the universities followed through by implementing such programs but on a miniscule scale that would not have any significant impact for decades.

While these problems altered both the perception and the reality of Japan as a superpower, the country remained a major player on the international scene but with a much lower profile. Japanese corporations have since remained among the top investors in assets abroad and continued to integrate their operations into the economies of China, East and Southeast Asia and elsewhere in the world.

However, the 1990s were watershed years for Japan's style of management, particularly among larger firms. The bursting of the so-called bubble economy in 1990 resulted in many companies breaking with tradition and either firing or forcibly retiring large numbers of employees, including managers and executives. Another trend—paying employees on a merit system rather than by seniority—became more common.

A third significant trend also became more pronounced: hiring mid-career people with special technical and marketing expertise away from other companies and in a few noteworthy occasions bringing in foreign executives in an effort to help salvage sinking firms.

Japanese management in both medium-and-large-scale enterprises has continued to evolve along Western lines, with some companies requiring the use of English as their official language. However, the government and most institutional organizations that are not directly involved in international competition and global relationships have changed very slowly if at all.

While the economy of the United States had benefitted greatly from imitating a number of Japanese business concepts during the 1970s and 1980s these benefits were undone in the first decade of the 21st century by a combination of intellectual failures and greed that gave precedence to profits in financial circles and among large corporations, and by a political quagmire that stifled initiative in the marketplace.

This American debacle also had a negative impact on the Japanese economy, and in 2011 this was compounded by an earthquake and a hugely destructive tsunami northeast of Tokyo that revealed more glaring weaknesses not only in many of Japan's top international corporations but also in the inept and politically divided Japanese government.

The public image of Japan that emerged in 2011 was one in which the government was dysfunctional and the economy was in dire straits—appearing very much like that of the United States. However, one of the characteristics the Japanese have always had is their ability to change their methods and their course rapidly in times of distress, and behind the scenes this trait had already kicked into over-drive.

By the end of 2011 there had been a dramatic change in the mindset and behavior of the Japanese in virtually all categories of industry and on all levels of management—a change based on the stark realization that the future of Japan depended on the rapid rationalization and globalization of both the economy and society in general.

Companies had begun recruiting young employees—Japanese and foreign—who were multi-lingual and multi-cultural. Some 40 percent of the employees of Sumitomo Chemical Company were non-Japanese. Virtually all of Japan's major international corporations had large recruiting programs in China. Even small shops catering to tourists had adopted a proactive global stance.

Another of the advantages of the Japanese was the ongoing hold the positive elements of their traditional culture had on the corporate world. Business management in Japan today is a hybrid of core concepts from the traditional culture and a growing number of Western business practices, and it is continuing to evolve.

There are a number of other significant factors that will help determine whether or not Japan remains a world-class economic power. One of these key factors is Japan's prowess in creating new technology. Another is entrepreneurship and a third is a wiser and more effective use of the female half of its workforce.

The technological prowess of the Japanese played a major role in the transformation of the country from an agrarian economy into a major industrial power in the 19th century, and will be a key to both the survival and progress of Japan in the future.

By 2011 just a few of the amazing technological advances that had begun to impact not only Japanese industry but the world at large included a process referred to as MEMS [Micro Electro Mechanical Systems], which had become a mainstay of companies that manufactured electronic components for automobiles, digital cameras, cell phones, gaming consoles, security systems and more.

In digital cameras, for example, MEMS technology makes it possible to take a perfectly clear image of a Bullet Train traveling at a speed of more than 250kph at dusk. A monitoring system in a room can detect a rise in a person's body temperature caused by a fever.

Another life-changing technology, created by Keio University Professor Susumu Tachi and his team in the Graduate School of Media Design, was a 3-D video system that makes it possible for people to see and communicate with each other in three dimensional environments, such as a Board Room, a café or living room—just like *Star Trek's* holodeck and devices used in *Star Wars* [in a universe far, far away!] for people in different galaxies to communicate with each other.

Already a leader in robotics technology, Japanese scientists had introduced a program that makes it possible for robots to learn on their own—without being programmed by humans. When a robot with this new technology encounters something in an environment that is not already in its "brain" it assimilates the new information. This will have incredible influence on virtually every aspect of human existence from now on.

Still another technological break-through was tiny generators that make electricity using ambient forms of heat, light and vibrations to power the devices they are in. In other words, rather than being just users of exlectricity these devices generate electricity; in some cases enough to make them self-powered. This technology can be incorporated into virtually anything affected by sunlight, temperature changes or vibrations, from buildings, floors, hallways, and sidewalks to highways.

Prior to the beginning of the 21st century Japan had one of the lowest rates of entrepreneurial activity among the world's leading nations—a situation that resulted from the fact that historically Japan had a cultural bias against entrepreneurship. During the long feudal Shogunate era [1192-1867] there were strong government sanctions against change that stifled the innovative and inventive spirit that is inherent in people.

The downfall of the Shogunate in 1867 and the following rapid industrialization of Japan removed many of the government barriers to this spirit and although the built-in cultural blocks are still very much in evidence today—big business and the regulatory environment continue to discourage business startups—things have changed.

Debbie Howard, president of Japan Market Resource Network [JMRN] and President Emeritus of the American Chamber of Commerce in Japan, noted that the shock of the 2011 earthquake, tsunami and melt-down of several nuclear reactors resulted in a spurt in the self-help and individualistic spirit of the Japanese but that alone was not enough to turn the economy around…a change, she says, that actually dated from 2004 by which time the people had lost faith in both big industry and the government because of 15 years of stagnation.

The entrepreneurial spirit of the Japanese has, in fact, been unleashed and is thriving among both the younger generations and displaced former company employees, and is playing an increasing role in Japan reinventing itself.

Howard went on to say that Japan could not and would not return to its glory days without removing the remaining barriers to women in the workplace—gender-based barriers that are still among the strongest in the leading countries despite some very visible progress. She pointed out that females make up approximately half of Japan's workforce but less than three percent of them are in managerial positions. She did not make the point—but could have—that Japanese females have been the leaders in virtually every cultural change outside of business and the government that has occurred in Japan since the late 1800s.

On the plus side, American and other Western companies with operations in Japan, unlike their Japanese counterparts, recognized the potential of female employees early, and have been leaders in taking advantage of the special mindset and skills of Japanese women.

Another major factor that is bringing increasing pressure on Japan's business and government leaders to continue transforming their traditional values and style of management is the changing of the social dynamics that began in the latter part of the 1980s when the melt-down of the economy started.

When corporate Japan began adopting American-style practices that diminished the workplace security of employees it dramatically eroded the relationships that had traditionally bound the Japanese in tight social networks, beginning with families, school ties and local communities.

The age at which young men and women married was soon extended by some 10 years; large numbers of single men and women began living alone; married women began having fewer children.

This transformation occurred in tandem with the growing emphasis on self-reliance, individuality, and the personal freedom that had never before existed in Japan—freedom that included self-indulgence on a massive scale, especially among young single women.

Now there are four Japans—the more traditional commercial enterprises, the high-tech startups, the government, and the population at large.

There are, in fact, five Japans—the fifth one comprised of hundreds of thousands of Buddhist and Shintō priests and their acolytes whose religious rituals and daily practices have not changed since ancient times; an equally large number of people who staff the country's hundreds of traditional inns and provide the same service and food—and dress in the traditional attire—that dates back to the 1600s. And then there are the hundreds of annual festivals that have not changed for up to 2,000 years; the thousands of artists and craftsmen whose methods have not changed since ancient times; and finally each year the hundreds of thousands of ordinary Japanese who don traditional garb and make religious pilgrimages on foot over routes that have been traveled since before the beginning of the Shogunate era in 1192.

All one has to do to re-enter the Old Japan—a 5th dimension if you will—that still exists is step through any of hundreds of thousands of doors to drinking establishments, inns, restaurants, entertainment halls, shops, temples and shrines that have retained their traditional character.

This book addresses key elements of the traditional culture that still apply to old-line companies and the government, and in varying degrees to most Japanese in all other aspects of society.

Given the track record of the Japanese in reinventing their economy in relatively short periods of time, and considering what Japanese companies are continuing to do to buttress their survival and growth, Japan cannot be ignored or counted out.

One of the most significant of these changes was a revolution in the distribution and retail trades. By 2005 company after company had begun moving much of their marketing and selling to the Internet. By 2012 online retailing was the fastest growth sector in the country.

A second factor that will play an increasingly important role in the viability of the Japanese economy was a rush by retail chains to open stores throughout Asia. Some companies have more locations overseas than they do in Japan. This new "soft" invasion by Japanese companies should not be taken lightly.

There are also aspects of Japan's traditional business culture that the United States and other countries around the world would do well to learn and adopt as quickly as possible.

These include the concepts and practices of *amae* [ah-my], *chishiki* [chee-she-kee], *kaizen* [kie-zen], *ninjo* [neen-joe], *shudan ishiki* [shuu-dahn ee-she-kee], and *tsukiai* [t'sue-kee-aye], explained in the text below.

Boyé Lafayette De Mente

PART 1

The Changing Face Of Japanese Business

To understand and deal effectively with the traditional management practices that continue to survive in present-day Japan's business world it is necessary to know the historical ethos of these practices and why they remain integral elements in the way the Japanese think and conduct business, including companies that have integrated a variety of Western concepts into their management practices.

All of the key elements of Japan's traditional business culture are bound up in and revealed in key words in the Japanese language—words that serve as windows to the essence of the culture and explain how these various elements have traditionally programmed the mindset and controlled the behavior of people.

While the power and role of many of these key words remain intact today, others have been modified by new realities of the times. Only a few of the terms have been discarded completely…and this almost always involves companies and people who are in "non-Japanese" situations and new technology that makes the human element secondary.

The traditional Japanese way of managing their enterprises was a merger of Shintō, Buddhist and Confucian concepts raised to the highest possible level and incorporating the physical, emotional, intellectual and spiritual aspects of life…things that went well beyond the Western concept of business management.

The heyday of this traditional Japanese way of doing business occurred in the 1970s, during which American and European business leaders once again descended upon Japan in huge numbers—*this time not to place more orders for cheap consumer goods but to try to find out why the Japanese were beating them at their own game!*

The question of why Japan was able to become the world's second-largest economic power in less than three decades (over and above the obvious factors of having had access to the rich markets and technology of the United States and Europe and outsourcing by the American military establishment for its wars in Korea and Vietnam) remains a fascinating and controversial subject.

In the 1970s, when the Japanese first began to feel obligated to come up with some kind of rationale for their achievements, many executives and commentators fixed on the traditional, glorified concept of *wa* (harmony) as the source of their success. This explanation was obviously not a complete answer, and a scramble began to come up with other reasons that were more specific and more believable.

These were the years when foreign business leaders first began to hear words like *kanban [kahn-bahn],* referring to just-in-time delivery of parts to assembly lines; *nemawashi* (behind-the-scenes consensus building or lobbying); *kaizen* (continuous improvement), and so on.

But even after these wonderfully insightful concepts were learned, there was still something missing. During the early years of the 1970s droves of American and European businesspeople trekked through hundreds of Japanese factories in an effort to glean some of the reasons for their remarkable productivity and product quality. It was reminiscent of another age [1952-1955] when it was Japanese managers, engineers, and technicians who flocked to the West on similar missions.

Verbal orientations that these foreign visitors received from their Japanese hosts invariably included claims that Japanese management and manufacturing processes were based on things they had learned from the United States in earlier decades. This always left the visitors feeling like they still were not being told the whole story. The briefings were also often laced with provocative but esoteric cultural concepts that further confused the visitors.

THE FOUNDATIONS OF JAPANESE BEHAVIOR

In factory after factory, the Western visitors found a level of order and cleanliness that was beyond their experience and expectations. Despite still gaping holes in their understanding of what made the Japanese such formidable competitors, this personal exposure was something like a Zen *koan* that shocked them into a degree of awareness. Some exclaimed in a burst of excited enlightenment, "Now I understand why the Japanese are so successful!"

Japanese managers and workers owe their passionate commitment to cleanliness and orderliness to Shintoism, which traditionally taught these traits to all Japanese as a major article of faith, and equated disorder and defilement with sin of the worst kind.

The traditions of ritualistic order and cleanliness remain a significant part of the character of the Japanee, and their conspicuous presence in Japanese factories today is nothing more than the continuation of age-old beliefs and practices that have distinguished the Japanese since the beginning of their civilization.

The concepts of orderliness and cleanliness that are characteristic of Japanese factories are embodied in five words that were practically enshrined as commandments: *shitsuke* (she-t'sue-kay), *seiri* (say-e-ree), *seiton* (say-e-tone), *seiketsu* (say-e-kate-sue), and *seisou* (say-e-so-uu).

Shitsuke means "training" and refers to the custom of factory managers rigorously training their employees in their job functions, their on-the-job behavior, and in total responsibility for the care of the workplace. *Seiri* means "orderliness" or everything in its prescribed place. *Seiton* means "neatness." *Seiketsu* means "cleanliness," and *seisou* refers to sweeping up dust—all clearly and precisely referring to a commitment that in many Western eyes verges on the obsessive.

One of the first things that Japanese managers of newly-bought foreign manufacturing companies generally did in the 1970s and 80s—much to the surprise of their foreign managers and employees—was instruct the employees of the plants to scrub and sweep the places until they were spotless. They were then instructed to put everything where it belonged.

The "five-S" factor in Japan's manufacturing industries goes well beyond its immediately visible manifestations. It is also indicative of a number of other traits that have contributed greatly to the success of the Japanese—from their conditioning in group behavior to their willingness to put the interests of the company above their own.

By the mid-1980s a number of American companies had, in fact, finally begun adopting elements from Japanese management concepts, particularly in design and quality control. But it was to take several years for these changes to show up in American products—even longer in the automobile industry, where *kaizen*, in particular, had finally become the mantra of GM, Ford, and other auto manufacturers.

As late as 1993 *TIME* magazine published a lead article noting that the leadership of the world's technological revolution had shifted from the U.S. to Japan, and that the Japanese had become "Oriental Vikings" who traveled the world, studying its many languages and plundering it for every new idea it could find.

But Japan remained the New Rome only until 2010 when it was overtaken by China. China passed Japan in economic size by imitating what the Japanese had done between 1870 and 1885 and again from 1948 to 1970…by becoming the world's top manufacturer of consumer goods at prices far lower than what they could be made in the U.S. and Europe—where most consumers were more concerned with price than with quality.

China's own rise to economic prominence did not begin until 1967 when Zedong Mao died and was replaced by Xiaoping Deng who changed the course of China with his capitalistic "To get rich is glorious!" policy.

Well before 2010 the Chinese had already replaced the Japanese as the world's most ubiquitous free-spending travelers, not only in the world at large but also in Japan itself, where they had become the mainstay of tourist oriented shops and services.

Another factor that played heavily on the beleaguered Japanese management system was the growing power of South Korean companies—which had virtually all of the strengths of traditional Japanese culture plus some unique characteristics of its own, and virtually none of Japan's weaknesses.

Unlike such things as Japan's consensus factor and harmony taking precedence over efficiency and expediency, Korean management was top-down, with powerful founders, their foreign-educated sons, and their equally autocratic managers calling the shots. In an incredibly short time such Korean companies as Samsung Electronics, LG Electronics and Hyundai Motor Corporation had joined the list of the world's top 100 brands.

By 2011 a number of Chinese companies had also begun to show up on lists of the most powerful and profitable brands in the world—a portent for the future that had far more implications than what either Japan or Korea represented.

The Social Media Factor
High-tech social media have played a significant role in reducing the inward looking stance of the Japanese and contributing to a global outlook in their mindset and behavior.

Facebook got off to a slow start when it was inaugurated in Japan in 2008 because of competing Japanese social sites like *mixi*, but things changed in 2010 when students and graduates of Japan's most prestigious universities began using the American site to search for jobs, resulting in several million users jumping onto the Facebook bandwagon.

Before the end of 2010 hundreds of Japanese companies had created Facebook accounts and were not only using major resources to promote and market their products on the Internet, they were mining Facebook as well as Twitter and blogs for leads in creating new products and improving existing ones.

A growing number of these companies had also begun to pitch their sales programs to international markets by presenting them in English and other languages. One of the most successful of these endeavors was newcomer high-mod apparel maker sg [slo, inc]; another was the well-known Uniqlo Co., whose combined Facebook fans was approaching two million.

When Nissan Motor Company introduced its new Leaf electric car in March 2010 its advertising was focused on the new social media, with staff assigned to personally respond to queries and comments from social media users.

Blogwatch Inc., a joint venture between Dentsu, Japan's largest advertising agency, and Recruit Co., Japan's largest human resources agency, had become a major player in extracting consumer data from social networks—further reflecting a seminal change in the business mindset and practices of the Japanese.

Facebook became even hotter as a result of its amazing role during and following the great earthquake and tsunami that struck the Fukushima area north east of Tokyo in the spring of 2011. The dramatic online images of the tsunami as it was coming in and then the devastation it caused made Facebook a household name.

The new users of Facebook were not put off by the fact that using the site required them to use their real names—something Japanese sites did not do and something the Japanese had previously been reluctant to do. That was a relatively minor but still significant change in Japanese culture, and Facebook has continued to play an important role in the Japanese becoming less ethnocentric and more open to the outside world.

However, despite these domestic and international factors and the ongoing changes in many of Japan's larger corporations, traditional attitudes and practices remain significant elements in their business etiquette and ethics.

The Introduction of "Learning Dormitories"
One of the social changes that resulted from the growing economic competition Japan faced from abroad and from the declining population was the introduction of modern condo-style co-ed dormitories on university campuses that were designed to attract Japanese as well as foreign students—a first in the history of the country.

The universities also eliminated the traditional hierarchy-based management system of the dorms, putting all residents on an equal footing and encouraging interaction among them to enhance cross-cultural exchanges and language learning. The condo-dorms at technical institutes were especially aimed at attracting more female students, whose numbers had historically been less than 10 percent of the student body.

The dorms include recreational and entertainment facilities and high-tech security systems.

Although further empowering the cultural changes that have been occurring in Japan since the 1990s overall the results of this new university policy will be slow in affecting management practices, especially in old-line companies and government ministries.

The English Language Challenge
Since most international business is conducted in the English language Japan's international business community faces a continuing challenge of increasing the number of English-speaking managers and engineers—and for both companies and universities to hire more foreigners who have new ideas as well as proficiency in English.

By the late 1990s many Japanese companies had begun to require some level of English proficiency in their new hires but these programs were not that successful and the number of foreigners employed by major corporations in managerial positions remained low. More dramatic action was needed.

In 2010 Rakuten Inc., Japan's largest internet retail seller, announced its intention of making English its official language, and gave its 7,000 employees until July 2012 to prepare for the full switch to English. Many of its employees who already spoke and used some English began crash programs to meet the language requirement.

Can anyone imagine an American company interested in doing business in China, for example, taking such a step? But it was indicative of the spirit and drive that resulted in war-devastated Japan becoming the second largest economy in the world between 1948 and 1970.

In many respects, however, the biggest language challenge Japan faces is not English. It is Japanese. One of the most important reasons why traditional elements in Japanese management have survived is the Japanese language itself.

Since languages are the repository and the transmitter of cultures, words in the Japanese language that are pregnant with cultural nuances and uses continue to influence the mindset and behavior of the Japanese, and are therefore keys to understanding the Japanese mind and behavior in business management.

In fact, the bedrock principles of Japanese life have traditionally been bound up in a number of special words that refer to a series of interrelated values, attitudes and practices that remain the basis of the etiquette and ethics in business, politics and professional organizations. Learning the cultural nuances and uses of these key terms is, in fact, the only way to fully understand the character of Japanese management.

Given the role of language in the attitudes and behavior of people *Nihongo* [Nee-hone-go], the Japanese language, it is not only the key to understanding Japanese attitudes and behavior, it is also the primary barrier foreigners face in understanding and dealing with the Japanese on an equal footing.

There are many Japanese today—the younger generations and those with international experience—who are less tied to the mindset and behavioral programming effects of the language. Others are also gradually discovering that they can escape the language-based cultural web that binds them to the Japanese way. But their numbers are still relatively small.

To give credit where it is due, hundreds of thousands of Japanese, particularly those going into international business, make a serious attempt to learn English. Private English language schools abound all over the country, and hundreds of companies retain foreign tutors for their employees and managers in their international divisions.

Almost all Japanese study English from two to eight years in public schools, and hundreds of thousand study English in private schools. Many of them will list English as something they have "accomplished," but only a small percentage of the population can converse even halfway fluently in the language or understand it when it is spoken to them. The reason is that most of their public school teachers could not speak English and therefore could not teach it properly as a spoken language.

While a tremendous amount of effort is still expended in reading English, it is generally read without benefit of knowing how to pronounce it properly. When read aloud or spoken it typically comes out "Japanized"—that is, broken down into Japanese syllables. The English word bread become "bu-re-do." Similarly, Mr. Smith becomes "Mi-su-ta Su-mi-su"; girl becomes "ga-ru"; and so on.

There is another unique factor in the Japanese language that is responsible for the influence it has on the Japanese mindset, on Japanese culture in general, and on many of the most positive attributes of the Japanese character, particularly those that have to do with the technical skills for which the Japanese are famous.

This linguistic factor [the preponderance of vowels in the language] results in the Japanese being primarily right-brain oriented [the emotional side] and secondarily left-brain oriented [the logical side]. This has resulted in them being forced to develop the ability to use both sides of their brain, making them more adept than most at thinking and acting holistically.*

---

*For more about this concept, see: *WHY THE JAPANESE ARE A SUPERIOR PEOPLE—The Advantages of Using Both Sides of Your Brain.*

Since only a few Western businesspeople speak Japanese fluently, and the majority of the Japanese speak little or no English or any other foreign language, the culture-laden language barrier causes many of the problems that beset Japanese and Westerners doing business with one another.

The Dangers in Using Interpreters
The use of English-speaking Japanese as interpreters is often not an adequate solution for non-Japanese speaking foreign businesspeople. Foreign executives have often related how they spent hours trying to convey something important to their Japanese counterparts through interpreters only to find their efforts wasted.

One such American, recently recounting an experience along this line, summed up the crux of the problem very aptly when he described the kind of interpreter that is needed when talking or negotiating with Japanese businesspeople. He said, "You need someone who can interpret thinking, not just words."

English-speaking Japanese interpreters used by foreign executives in Japan are often young, have had little or no business experience themselves, are likely to be inadequately experienced in handling cross-cultural human relations problems (which is always a big part of interpreting), and are almost always called upon to interpret to older, higher ranking Japanese executives.

In their efforts to avoid creating awkward situations these interpreters habitually water down the foreigner's remarks to avoid upsetting the Japanese side. They must also avoid the *gaijin kusai* [guy-jeen kuu-sie], or "smelling like a foreigner" syndrome.

Foreign executives commonly assume that a Western-educated Japanese employee, interpreter, friend, or contact who speaks adequate if not fluent English is a "friend" in an "enemy camp" who can be depended upon to carry out their instructions and wishes fully. While each case has to be considered individually, this is often not so. There are a number of interesting reasons why it is not so.

First and most important, if Western-educated Japanese are in a medium-sized or larger organization, and especially if they are not one of the top executives, they are up against a system that takes priority over personality and character factors, and despite their foreign veneer they are still very much a part of that system.

Foreign-educated Japanese employees naturally tend to become buffers between foreigners and their Japanese superiors and coworkers. When they speak to the foreigner, they put on their Western veneer and understand and sympathize with the foreigner. When they turn around and speak to their Japanese colleagues and seniors, the system de-mands that they become one of them and do their best to see the foreigner through Japanese eyes.

Because of such problems, it is usually wiser for foreigners to employ older persons as interpreters—even when their English language proficiency may be less than that of a young person who may have studied abroad. The greater social status of the older individual will often more than compensate for a lesser ability in English.

Foreign executives who want to further balance the scales in their favor by engaging the services of older interpreters of recognized social and economic rank should explain to the interpreters that their status, knowledge, and experience are needed to offset the foreigners' lack of understanding of local customs.

This said, during the first decade of the 21st entury the whole language/interpreter problem began to diminish somewhat as more and more Japanese companies began hiring more foreigners for their Japan operations [mostly Chinese, Koreans and other Asians] as well as directly recruiting Japanese who were studying in the U.S. and the U.K.

A larger than normal percentage of these new hires were female because senior Japanese managers had learned that females are generally better linguists than males and are more likely to be both loyal and diligent—something that American companies operating in Japan had already learned.

Advances in technology will no doubt dramatically reduce the problems that have traditionally resulted from linguistic and cultural barriers between the Japanese and the outside world. The challenge will be for these *Star Trek*-like communicators to include the cultural content of the languages concerned.

As noted earlier, foreign businesspeople—and others in general—who want to fully understand the Japanese and their culture must start with key terms in the Japanese language that are pregnant with cultural content, keeping in mind that the nuances and use of some of the most important of these words are changing with the times, presenting an ongoing challenge.

As late as 2012 a headline in Japan's leading economic journal announced that when it came to communicating on a global scale Japanese corporations were still "tongue-tied."

THE FOUNDATIONS OF JAPANESE BEHAVIOR

One important cultural factor that is generally overlooked when considering the challenges the Japanese face in communicating in English fully and effectively is that they must learn how to *think* in English; not just be able to use the English equivalents of Japanese words. The essence and nuances of words are based on the culure in which the language developed. The Japanese word for sincere [seijitsu] goes far beyond the English word sincere, and this difference is true for most of the culturally pregnant words in the two languages.

And there is another factor in the language dilemma the Japanese face. Older Japanese in particular do not want to give up the unique Japanese spirit that is incorporated in their language. They do not want to lose the advantage it gives them.

PART 2
Traditional Elements In Japan's Business Culture

Despite ongoing changes in the Japanese way of doing business elements of Japan's traditional culture remain primary factors in most areas of management. As noted earlier, these factors evolved from ancient Shintō, Buddhist and Con-fucian concepts that created the distinctive character and personality of the Japanese, and were honed to perfection by the strict code of the samurai who ruled the country from 1192 until 1867. The foundation of Japan's traditional cul-ture was based on the Shintō concept of a harmonious rela-tionship with all things in nature.

Wa
[Wah]
The Foundation of Japanese Behavior

It was not until well into the 1970s that Japanese businessmen really accepted the idea that there was indeed something unique in their culture that gave them a significant economic advantage over Western nations, and it was not until the early 1980s that they began to feel at ease and confident in attributing their remarkable accomplishments to such traditional concepts as *wa* [wah].

Then, suddenly, *wa* was on the lips of almost all executives who got up before any kind of audience, including their own employees, because here was a concept, sanctified by age, that they could really get their teeth into. It was endlessly pointed out that *wa,* the ancient word for the concept of peace and harmony, literally means "circle" and that the secret of Japan's economic success was based on employees and managers functioning in human-oriented "circles" instead of the series of horizontal layers favored by Western management. [In ancient times the Chinese word for Japan was Wa.]

Thereafter the principle of *wa* in all of its various nuances was given credit for almost every aspect of Japanese management that had proven effective. As manager after manager explains, *wa* incorporates mutual trust between management and labor, unselfish cooperation between management and labor, harmonious relations among employees on all levels, unstinting loyalty to the company, mutual responsibility, job security, freedom from competitive pressure from other employees, and collective responsibility for both decisions *and* results—much of which was never totally true in all circumstances but it was the ideal and was pursued with diligence.

Wa was also said to be responsible for such things as the almost total lack of joking, horse-playing, complaining, drinking on duty, and other nonproductive behavior in Japanese companies. It was also responsible for the active participation of assembly line workers in the management process through such techniques as *Jishu Kanri* Jee-shuu Kahn-ree), or "Volunteer Management" groups. Each of these groups was made up of about ten workers who met regularly to discuss their work, as well as the jobs of those around them that impinged on their own output. Then they made suggestions to management for improvements.

The concept of *wa* provided the Japanese with an all-in-one philosophy/ethic for their business system that included specific

THE FOUNDATIONS OF JAPANESE BEHAVIOR

day-to-day guidelines. Furthermore, it was a system of thought and behavior that they did not have to go to business schools or seminars to learn because it was part of their culture.

However, beginning in the 1980s many major firms started requiring new employees to take intense courses in the principles and practices of *wa* to make up for the fact that they were no longer being programmed in wa either in their homes or in schools.

There is nothing mysterious or esoteric about the *wa* that still exists in Japan. It is nothing more than a deeply ingrained system of principles and rules designed to prevent conflict and to promote harmony, mutual trust, mutual help, mutual respect, cooperation, and so on—all traits with which Westerners have a nodding acquaintance. But there are profound differences in the way Japanese and Westerners do business. The most important of these differences is that the Japanese system, as inhuman as it can sometimes be, is based on human feelings and needs and is intensely personal.

Konosuke Matsushita, founder of Matsushita/Panasonic fame, one of largest manufacturers of consumer electronics, was widely regarded in Japan as the supreme master of the "Way of Wa." Before retiring from the chairmanship of his company in the 1970s, Matsushita codified his *wa* approach to management in seven objectives which each Matsushita employee was expected to learn and follow. These objectives were: 1. National Service through Industry; 2. Harmony; 3. Cooperation; 4. Struggle for Betterment; 5. Courtesy and Humility; 6. Adjustment and Assimilation; 7. Gratitude.

One can begin to grasp how important these concepts were to Matsushita managers and workers—and in considerable degree to all Japanese businesspeople and workers—by equating them with the role of the Ten Commandments in the Christian religion, keeping in mind that the Japanese tended to take Matsushita's guidelines seriously.

Businesspeople as "Living Buddhas"

To fully understand Japanese management practices and deal effectively with Japanese businesspeople requires more than a surface knowledge of the concept of *wa*. It requires an intimate familiarity with the Japanese character and work ethic as they have been fashioned by one of the world's most extraordinary cultures.

Japanese writer, publisher and biblical scholar Shichihei Yamamoto credits a 16th century Zen priest, Shosan Suzuki, with being responsible for the development of capitalism in Japan. He also views Baigan Ishida, a 17th century store clerk turned-economic-philosopher, as the man who expanded on Suzuki's views to develop the economic philosophy and work ethic that still survives in present-day Japan.

In his book *Nihon Shihon-shugi no Seishin (The Spirit of Japanese Capitalism),* Yamamoto says that Suzuki (1579-1655) taught a Zen-based social ethic in which people had to become "living Buddhas" in order to live the way he felt they should. He preached that work equaled asceticism and was in itself an expression of religious piety. He taught that an unbendable commitment to honesty was the first article of faith for businesspeople. He saw commerce, which was considered a necessary evil by the Shogunate government of feudal Japan, as a godly endeavor whose primary goal was to bring freedom to the nation.

A former samurai and government official, Suzuki expressed the desire to conquer the world with Buddhist law, with his social ethic becoming the basis for all societies and serving as a national morality that would satisfy the spiritual, religious, and economic needs of all people. In Suzuki's philosophy businesspeople who pursue their trade to make a profit will fail. It is only by keeping the needs of the consumers and the nation in the forefront of all thinking, planning, and working that one can succeed. Otherwise, he adds, that person will incur the wrath of Buddha.

Yamamoto says Japanese salespeople who started going abroad in the 1960s did indeed look and act like religious pilgrims as they trekked the world with their samples and sales pitches and treated commerce like an ascetic exercise.

In this view the reason the Japanese were, and for the most part still are, such hard, dedicated workers was because *work* was their religion, and in Yamamoto's view it was this religious attitude toward work that was behind Japan's economic success.

From 1952 to 1990 the Japanese were, in fact, filled with the fever of true religious zealots in their efforts to achieve greater and greater economic goals. Probably few, if any, Japanese would admit that part of their motivation may indeed have been a subconscious desire to achieve Buddhahood, but they would certainly understand and appreciate the concept.

There are several dozen key words in the Japanese lexicon that are the building blocks of *wa,* words that define and explain in copious detail the traditional beliefs and behavior of the Japanese. Without an understanding and appreciation of these terms, the portrait of Japan's business system is little more than a shadow.

Amae
[Ah-my]
The Building Blocks of Wa

The foundation of Japanese *wa* [harmony] is based on the concept and practice of *amae* [ah-my]. *Amae* is translated as "indulgent love," the category and quality of love an infant feels for an absolutely kind and loving mother *and must have from its mother to stay right with the world!*

The principle and practice of *amae* are certainly not unique to Japan, but the Japanese are apparently the only people (other than perhaps isolated tribes or islanders) who made it the primary essence of their distinctive social system.

In his authoritative book *Amae no Kozo,* published in English as *The Anatomy of Dependence,* Takeo Doi, one of Japan's leading psychiatrists, observed that while *amae* is the "oil of life" in Japan, the principle is generally unrecognized in the West, even though it is one of the fundamental building blocks of human (and animal!) personality.

In practical terms, the Japanese do not feel comfortable or right in any person-to-person relationship that does not include *amae.* By this, they mean a feeling of complete trust and confidence, not only that the other party will not take advantage of them, but also that they—in business or in private life—can presume upon the indulgence of the other.

All people, says Doi, have a deep, innate desire to unload their troubles on someone they can trust, on someone from whom they can receive recognition and advice. In other words, we need someone who will relieve us of our excess psychic baggage.

In Doi's concept, it is the person who can safely encourage infantile dependence *(amae)* in its purest form who is most qualified to be elevated to a position of leadership in Japan. Leaders, being utterly dependent on those beneath them, are least likely to mislead those people because the leaders would be hurting themselves.

The *amae* factor in Japanese psychology, according to Doi's line of reasoning, is what accounts for the "childish" behavior often ascribed to Japanese adults.

Expressed in another way, *amae (amaeru)* means "to mother" and "to be mothered"—referring specifically to the purest form of ego-less relationship between a loving mother and an absolutely trusting infant. Without *amae* in infancy and childhood, notes Doi, the child's psyche and personality are scarred for life.

In Western societies, growing up has traditionally been related to *repressing* the need for *amae* and eventually giving up its practice—a factor that is obviously the key to some of the profound differences between Western and Japanese attitudes and behavior, since they emphasize *amae* throughout life.

Doi proposes that the *amae* mentality of the Japanese goes back to their primal experience during the dawn of their history. Furthermore, he adds, it was national policy until the beginning of the modern era. He says that the traditional Japanese concept of peace and harmony *(wa),* which many older Japanese still feel Japan is obligated to spread to the rest of the world, is nothing more than "idealized *amae.*

In all of their business deals the Japanese still seek to establish an *amae* relationship that entails trust and confidence in the behavior and goals of the other parties.

THE FOUNDATIONS OF JAPANESE BEHAVIOR

Kata
[Kah-tah]
The Role of "Form" in Japanese Behavior

From around the sixth century A.D. to well after the beginning of the modern era in 1867, the Japanese were more concerned with *kata* [kah-tah], the form or way of doing things, than sincerity or accomplishment. The people were required to walk a certain way, to move their hands a certain way, to open doors a certain way, to sleep with their head pointing in a certain direction and to arrange their legs a certain way. The style and manner of their dress was prescribed by law for several generations before the beginning of the modern era. Their manner of eating was severely prescribed; they could enter a house only a certain way and greet each other only a certain way. Even physical movements necessary to perform many types of work were definitively established and no deviation was allowed.

So rigid and so severe were these prescribed manners that they long ago became a part of the Japanese personality, permeating and shaping every phase and facet of their lives, and were passed on from one generation to the next. Today most foreigners doing business in Japan quickly learn that there is still a Japanese way to do virtually everything as a result of this meticulous conditioning over the centuries.

Class, sex, age, family ties, and previous dealings determined the behavior of the Japanese in every area of their lives. Form and manner, the outward expressions of the system, were sanctified as virtues. The extent to which this stratified and categorized society developed in Japan would be unbelievable if it were not for the fact that it is still present today, especially in the professional and business world, in somewhat diluted form.

Business and other relations in Japan have traditionally been conducted within the web of this etiquette system, based on personal obligations owed to others. All dealings were and still are conducted within a set of rules that were designed to prevent trouble and to prevent or control change. For ages perfect hierarchical harmony at virtually any human cost was Japan's *Golden Rule*.

THE FOUNDATIONS OF JAPANESE BEHAVIOR

Today, the businessperson in Japan reflects centuries of conditioning in harmony in many ways—dread of personal responsibility; preference for mutual cooperation and group effort; tendency to follow the mass and to imitate success; reluctance to oppose anyone openly; and desire to submerge individualism into larger surroundings. As a result of this conditioning, individual Japanese have been the ideal corporate employee for over a thousand years.

A further result of the enforcement of Japan's *Golden Rule* of *wa* [wah], and a factor that still makes it possible to generalize about Japanese businesspeople with an astonishing degree of accuracy, is their mental homogeneity. As early as the 10th century Japanese society had already developed into a highly specialized, intense, and uniform civilization in which the people dressed alike within their class, were subjected to the same experiences, and had the same stock of knowledge and same prejudices.

This sameness was so pervasive that, according to cultural historians, ordinary means of communication were unnecessary. The Japanese were so attuned to one another's attitudes and manners that the slightest hint or gesture was sufficient to convey their meaning with an almost magical facility.

It is not hard to understand the reasons for this extraordinary similarity of the Japanese. First, there was nearly complete isolation from the rest of the world for the first several thousand years of their history. Second, the small inhabited land area of the islands resulted in all the various influences that shaped the culture being felt at about the same time and more or less evenly by all the people.

Obviously there have been significant changes in the mindset and behavior of most Japanese born since the 1960s, but even the maverick younger generations must adjust to a considerable extent to the institutionalized attitudes and rules governing corporations, organizations and government entities.

But the future of of both *wa* and *amae* in Japan are being weakened by globalization of the Japanese economy and the imperative that Japanese management learn how to compete with foreign managers on the same level. By the first decade of the 21st century the new business mantra was that Japanese managers must learn how to think and act individually, and pressure was being placed on universities to teach that kind of thinking and acting. However, that kind of fundamental change in an institutionalized and coded culture cannot take place quickly.

For a definitive analysis of the Kata factor in Japanese behavior, see *KATA—The Key to Understanding and Dealing with the Japanese* [Tuttle Publishing].

Makoto
[Mah-koe-toe]
Sincerity, Japanese Style

It is not unusual for both Japanese and Western executives to accuse each other of being insincere and sometimes dishonest. What neither side appreciates is that in most cases they are referring to entirely different concepts of sincerity and honesty.

In many situations, the Japanese idea of right and wrong is quite different from the Western idea. To the typical Japanese, right or wrong is not so much based on an unvarying, universal code of ethics or principles as it is upon time, place, the people involved, and other circumstances. The Japanese concept of justice is subsequently not as abstract as the Western idea.

I once attended a large reception staged in Tokyo by the importing division of an American company for Hitachi Ltd., one of their suppliers, and several guests of note. There were a number of speeches by Hitachi executives, and in every case the speaker not only began and ended his talk with an appeal to the Americans to be sincere in their dealings with them but also harped on this point throughout his speech.

Catching the spirit of the thing, some of the American speakers countered and asked the Japanese to also be sincere. An outsider would probably have thought these were spontaneous demonstrations of goodwill in which both parties were talking about the same thing and were really communicating with one another. But sincerity as used by the Japanese has altogether a different meaning than it does to Westerners. And it is of course vitally important to understand this difference when doing business with Japanese.

Sincerity to most Westerners means free from pretense or deceit; iIn other words, honest and truthful without reservations. But to the typical Japanese, being *makoto* (mah-koe-toe) means to properly discharge all of one's obligations so that everything will flow smoothly and harmony will be maintained. It also means being careful not to say or do anything that would cause loss of face. By extension, it further means that *makoto* people will not be self-seeking; will not get excited or provoke others to excitement; will not reveal their innermost thoughts if they are negative; will not, in fact, do anything disruptive.

This, obviously, does not necessarily include or require strict adherence to what Westerners like to call honesty and frankness, since harmony of a kind can be maintained indefinitely as long as both sides play according to the same rules. And the Japanese, just like the Westerners, tend to think and behave as if their rules were the ones being used.

Japanese businesspeople, as mentioned earlier, often seem to be more concerned with form and manner than they are with the end results of any effort, although results are, of course, important to them. Since this attitude is nearly the opposite of typical Western thinking it naturally causes varying degrees of misunderstanding and friction between the parties involved.

Japanese still tend to think in terms of personal relationships and subjective circumstances in their business dealings. Thus an agreement between Japanese and foreign businesspeople should be reduced to its basic elements, and each point should be thoroughly discussed to make sure both sides understand and actually agree to what the other side is saying.

But reaching an agreement with a Japanese company does not mean the foreign company is home free. From the instant the agreement is made or signed, the interests of the two parties will begin to diverge. The agreement will be interpreted differently by the two sides, and unless there is ongoing "root binding" and nurturing of the agreement by face-to-face dialogue and adjustments, the interests of the two parties are likely to be so far apart within two or three years that the relationship goes sour.

This usually happens, not because of dishonesty or deviousness on the part of either party, but simply because of differences in the perceptions and reactions of the two parties. Among other things, it is the Japanese position that since circumstances change regularly, it is natural that contractual relationships between companies also change regularly.

One of the major weaknesses of American executives dealing with Japan, particularly in joint ventures, is their failure to recognize and react positively to the constant need to nurture and adjust their relationships with their Japanese partners.

Shinyo
[Sheen-yoh]
Trust in the Way of Wa

Westerners have often commented on how difficult it is to develop a close personal relationship with Japanese businesses, especially in a short period of time. Besides the communication and other cultural barriers that usually separate the two sides, the Japanese are reluctant to extend their friendship to anyone with whom they do not have *shinyo* (sheen-yoh)—trust, confidence, faith. To the Japanese, a person in whom they can have *shinyo* has a sense of honor and will do what is expected whatever the cost.

The development of *shinyo* comes about only as a result of a successful *amae* relationship with another person that takes years. Foreigners who do business in Tokyo on a two-or three-year assignment or less cannot expect to establish close, personal ties with their Japanese colleagues that transcend either their foreignness or their professional roles.

The *amae* relationship, involving the child-parent-adult personalities in each individual, is a kind of game the Japanese play in all walks of life, between subordinates and superiors and sometimes between equals as well. Each individual has to know which role is proper for what situation, who can legitimately play that role and how it should be played.

Foreigners doing business in Japan have generally had no experience at playing the parent role with employees (or the child role if they are approaching senior Japanese business executives), and are usually unable to establish the kind of rapport the Japanese expect and feel comfortable with. As a result, there is almost always an undercurrent of tension in employee-management relations in Japanese/foreign firms and in meetings between Japanese and Westerners.

By the same token, Japanese managers stationed abroad often find that they can no longer play the parent role smoothly, even with Japanese subordinates working under them. The system simply doesn't work well outside the cultural context of Japan. Where foreign employees of overseas Japanese operations are concerned, Japanese managers either keep their distance or do their best to play the adult-to-adult role in an awkward situation for most because they usually have not had experience in adult-adult relationships with subordinates.

When pressed to go beyond *wa* to explain the high productivity rate of their factories, Japanese managers will often refer to the *shinyo,* or trust, that exists between Japanese workers and managers and between companies and unions. This trust is easy enough to define but difficult to copy. It is an integral and inseparable part of the Japanese system of virtually guaranteed lifetime employment among major firms, long-term on-the-job training, promotions and pay raises.

The management system in most Japanese companies is still primarily based on seniority, collective decision-making, mutual responsibility and a degree of company loyalty that transcends most personal considerations. It also gives young managers training in several departments instead of requiring them to specialize. Managers are, as a result, generally not isolated from workers and have traditionally been held as responsible for the emotional well-being of their employees as they are for their professional and technical competence.

Fundamental cultural differences make it impossible for Western businesspeople to adopt the *shinyo* system completely in their management practices. However, some of the tenets are easily adaptable to any enterprise, such as the training programs that make it possible for managers to have faith in both the ability and integrity of employees.

Westerners wanting to do business in Japan or already doing business there would do well to stress that they understand and agree with the role of *shinyo* in business relationships and that it is also part of their culture.

Uramu
[Uu-rah-muu]
That Hostile Feeling

When the typical Japanese employee's efforts to *amaeru* are ignored or rebuffed, he or she will generally be upset. In fact, Doi says that when the Japanese are unable to express their *amae,* the essential ingredient for the development of trust and faith in another person, a type of hostility called *uramu* (uu-rah-muu) emerges. This hostility, he explains, is manifested by a deep-seated feeling of resentment against the person or system involved.

Younger Japanese are not likely to be upset by the lack of *amaeru* in their relationships with foreign coworkers or employers because they know it is a Japanese thing. However, they respond to it positively because it touches on human feelings that cross all cultural barriers—as long as it is not smothering.

Here again, knowledge of the *uramu* factor in the makeup of most Japanese and doing the things necessary to prevent it from arising is one of the elements for success in Japan.

Enryo
[In-ree-oh]
Holding Back

When the Japanese do not feel comfortable with someone or something—that is, when they cannot practice *amae*—they practice *enryo* (in-ree-oh), literally, "considering (things) from a distance." This is a word heard frequently in Japan, usually as *"Go-enryo-naku"*(go-in-ree-oh-nah-kuu), or "Please don't hold-back, don't be shy."

Many Japanese claim that they do not like to *enryo* themselves but they expect others to do it. The Japanese *enryo* a great deal, however, because it is their customary way of opposing things or avoiding situations that might result in incurring unwanted obligations or in disrupting harmony.

In most business relations with people who are still more or less strangers the Japanese feel constrained to practice *enryo* because there are always barriers between people who do not have an *amae* relationship!

Westerners generally do not or cannot verbalize the concept of *amae* the way the Japanese do because we do not have a specific, commonly known and used word for it. We are able to practice *amae* to a shallow but nevertheless important degree toward almost anyone, however, often immediately after meeting them.

Traditionally, adult Japanese tended to either ignore both other Japanese who were strangers and the outside world, or maintain a guarded stance toward them because their ability to feel and practice *amae* with others was based on long-term, face-to-face relationships.

Earle Okumura, a veteran consultant on doing business in Japan, uses two variable concentric figures (Figures 1 and 2) to illustrate the basic differences in the psychology and personality of Japanese and Westerners.

Westerners, as shown in Figure 1, have a large, thick inner core (psyche), with a thin, easily penetrable outer shell. On the other hand, the Japanese (Figure 2) have a small, fragile inner core (psyche), with two other barriers designed to keep people at a distance. The first barrier is thick and strong; the second one is conspicuously thin and fragmentary.

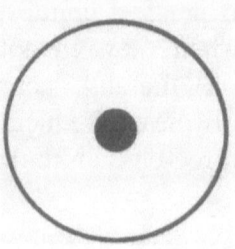

THE FOUNDATIONS OF JAPANESE BEHAVIOR

Figure 1 / Westerner

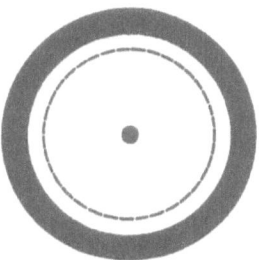

Figure 2 / Japanese

As the images indicate, it is easy to approach a Westerner and get on relatively close terms in a short period of time—often within minutes. At the same time, however, the massive, solid core of the Westerner prevents the individual from really opening up, from dropping all barriers to the inner self. No matter how close Westerners may come, even husbands and wives, few of them can truthfully say they know the other person fully. There are invariably dark areas of doubt and wonder.

In contrast, the thick outer barrier surrounding the Japanese makes it difficult and time consuming to establish an initial relationship. But once the heavy protective guard is penetrated, the psyche of the Japanese is fully exposed and extremely vulnerable to the unscrupulous person. The Japanese have traditionally been understandably wary of letting anyone inside their personal sphere.

However, there have been remarkable changes in this aspect of the Japanese character beginning soon after the end of World War II in 1945. Programming in the homes and schools was no longer rigidly based on the traditional cultural themes because most of what the Japanese had believed was the sources of their spiritual strength and prowess had proven false.

While the concept and practice of *enryo* survived over the decades it became less and less important to the younger generations, and then a remarkable natural disaster happened in the spring of 2011 that was to have an astounding impact on public displays of *enryo*—the earthquake and the great tsunami that followed it that devasted the Fukushima area of northeast of Tokyo.

Prompted by searing images of the disaster millions of Japanese—many for the first time in their lives—voiced strong criticism of corporate managers and government officials for their inadequate responses to the tragedy. This event marked a change in the *enryo*-based restraints on the public behavior of the Japanese, and will surely continue to influence their private and professional behavior as well.

For a very precise picture of what this cultural change would do to the Japanese all one has to do is consider the behavior of Koreans. They do not *enryo*.

Giseisha
[Ghee-say-e-shah]
The Victim Syndrome

The *amae* expectations of many Japanese, especially older generations, instill in them a strong tendency to be come dependent on others and they suffer from a built-in susceptibility to emotional injury—expressed by the term *giseisha* (ghee-say-e-shah)—when their expectations are not met. They experience this "victim syndrome" whenever anybody or anything hinders or interferes with their aims or efforts. This feeling is most likely to be triggered when someone, some company, or some country on which they have been passively dependent, does something they feel is against their interests.

This "victim mentality," carries with it an underlying need to get revenge to wipe out the "insult." Japanese history is filled with incidents of revenge carried out by people who had been slighted or blocked, and in earlier times there was a Shogunate provision that gave individuals the legal right to carry out a vendetta attack against those who had wronged them, including killing those who were guilty.

Amae-based revenge today is far more subtle, and may be spread out over a long period of time. The only way to avoid this syndrome is to be sensitive enough to recognize that a slight or some kind of disappointment has occurred and deal with it directly and quickly by explaining why it happened, apologizing for the action, and promising to make up for it in the future.

Japanese managers in foreign companies who feel slighted or blocked in their aspirations by their foreign overseers, or regard the foreigners as incompetent, have historically mounted campaigns to get the foreign executives called home or fired.

One of the ways for foreigners to become aware and stay aware of such undercurrents among their Japanese managers is to regularly take individuals and small groups of the employees out for dining and drinking sessions. It is almost always only in convivial afterhours drinking sessions that the Japanese will reveal their true feelings...which is one of the primary reasons why there are so many bars and cabarets in Japan.

Chokkan to Roni
[Choke-kahn toh Roan-ree]
Intuition vs. Logic

It is sometimes said that Japanese businesspeople use *Jan-Ken-Pon* [Jahn-Kane-Pone) logic. *Jan-Ken-Pon* refers to the popular paper-scissors-stone game played with the hands and fingers, especially by the young, to settle questions or points of order. In this context, it refers to logic that is cyclic or elastic, not absolute.

In general terms, Japanese thinking tends to be intuitive instead of logical, which Doi explains in terms of *amae*. Of course, intuitive thinking is not necessarily or always undesirable. The management philosophy followed by Konosuke Matsushita, founder of the huge Matsushita Electric Corporation (now Panasonic), and many of Japan's other most successful business leaders, includes the use of intuitive intelligence.

Part of the intuitive process of this unique management philosophy is expressed in the term *kongen* (kone-gain), which more or less means "the root of the universe." It refers to the energy that fuels the universal-energy-wisdom that can be tapped by meditating, by emptying one's conscious mind of all thoughts and thereby opening it to communication with cosmic consciousness. Matsushita, who was regarded by many as the greatest Japanese business executive of modern times, credited *kongen* as the source of his management philosophy. Following his example, top Matsushita executives meditated regularly...and some still do.

There are also many positive aspects of the practice of *amae*. It emphasizes tolerance, nondiscrimination, and equality. It also allows the Japanese to accept, absorb, and assimilate non-threatening new ideas—technical, social, or philosophical—without internal conflicts.

The deep, compelling urge the Japanese have to *amae* may also be responsible for the powerful desire they have for knowledge. Anything that is unfamiliar or unknown to them, and therefore making an *amae* relationship impossible, represents an unacceptable threat. It is characteristic of the Japanese, when faced with something new, to say, "We must learn everything there is to know about it in order to protect ourselves, and if there is anything worthwhile in the new thing we will adapt it to our own uses."

Foreigners who demonstrate awareness of these elements in Japanese culture have a much better chance for getting along with their Japanese counterparts and employees.

Shudan Ishiki
[Shuu-dahn Ee-she-kee]
All Together Now

Most top Japanese business executives tend to be philosophers, very much concerned with the morality of the Japanese enterprise system and its perpetuation. One of the ways they attempt to achieve their purpose is to promote a type of group-thinking called *shudan ishiki* (shuu-dahn ee-she-kee). This way of thinking emphasizes the functions and goals of the group, as opposed to thinking in terms of experience, qualifications, and responsibilities of the individual. It has, of course, long been an ideal of Japanese society.

Virtually all of the training programs sponsored by Japanese corporations, both intellectual and physical, are designed to enhance *shudan ishiki*, which incorporates all of the premises of

THE FOUNDATIONS OF JAPANESE BEHAVIOR

wa, amae, kata and the other foundations of traditional Japanese culture.

Foreign executives in Japan and working with Japan should, of course, be aware of the *shudan ishiki* theme and include it in their presentations and practices.

On
[Own]
The Web that Binds

Within the context of the traditional Japanese social system and its emphasis on *wa,* the key word was *on* (own), which refers to the various obligations—to themselves, to each other, their clan or country, and to the world—that until recent times all Japanese were automatically assigned at birth or that they incurred during their lifetime.

These various obligations, all designed to maintain peace and harmony within the confines of the superior-subordinate system, formed the principles on which Japan's extraordinary society grew. This was a society that was built upon a class and ranking system in which position and severely prescribed manners, rights, and responsibilities were absolute values that were imposed upon the people with relentless power.

As long as they remained members of their society, the preindustrial Japanese were not free to say anything, take any action, or have any thought that was not prescribed by the dictates of their position and by the *on* adhering to that position. A Japanese could not (and in many situations still cannot!) even say "sit down" without using words that properly denoted his position in life in relation to the person addressed. In bowing, the Japanese had to know when to bow, how low to bow, how long the bow should be maintained, and how many times to bow.

It may be difficult for the Western mind to grasp just how important these manners were to the early Japanese. Westerners are generally conditioned to conduct their lives according to certain abstract principles, with manners playing only a minor role. In Japan, the emphasis was reversed and a social system was forged in which the ultimate virtue was a prescribed conduct. Morality [ethics] was primarily an aspect of day-to-day manners; not a philosophical or religious concept.

An understanding of this theme in Japanese culture can help foreigners understand Japanese behavior that does not appear to fit the circumstances, or that appears to be in excess or extreme for the situation at hand.

Giri
[Ghee-ree]
The Personal Code

One is not likely to hear the term *giri* [ghee-ree] in ordinary discourse in Japan today—except among *yakuza* gang members—but the concept remains discernible in virtually every category of Japanese life, and particularly so in business, government agencies and professional organizations.

While *on* may be said to be the universal obligation the Japanese traditionally accrued as a result of being born, raised, educated and employed, *giri* (ghee-ree) is the personal code, the deep sense of duty, of honor that compels them to fulfill their obligations—for good or bad.

Both *on* and *giri* are reciprocal in nature and derive from a relationship in which the subordinate is expected to extend service and loyalty to the superior, and the superior is obligated to demonstrate responsibility and gratitude to the subordinate. Without *giri,* the *on* system would disintegrate.

In earlier times this Japanese code of honor was often referred to as "*giri* to one's name." Failure to keep *giri* to one's name results in loss of face. Westerners are, of course, familiar with the idea of losing face because the words and the idea have been bandied about since the turn of the twentieth century. But few appreciate the significance of the term or how important the idea of losing face is to everyday business and social life in Japan [and in Korea and China]. To lose face means much more to the Japanese than simply being embarrassed or insulted.

Although such sensitivity to all outside influences is a handicap for the Japanese, it is not something they can take off like a coat. It is part of their national character. It is especially important for people who have professional status of any kind or degree to protect their face.

Maintaining their face or reputation as a professional person does not mean, however, that they have to be skilled in their line of work or conduct themselves ethically. It means, instead, that they cannot, in *giri* to their name, admit ignorance or inability or allow anyone to besmirch their name without serious consequences to their self-image and sense of well-being.

This aspect of Japanese culture often creates situations that Westerners do not expect and do not understand. It can be especially critical in business and political negotiations. However, the more Westernized the Japanese have become and the less beholden they are to any Japanese group, the less power *giri* has on their behavior.

The concept of *giri* is, of course, known in the West and plays a role in the lives of people, but it has never been as institutionalized or as ritualized as it was in Japan. And because it was so ingrained in the mindset of the Japanese, and despite its negative elements, it played a positive role in the rise of Japan as a superpower by compelling most Japanese to work harder and with more diligence than other people.

Ninjo
[Neen-joe]
Human Feelings Come First

Giri without human guidelines would have been unthinkable for the Japanese. These were provided by other principles within the framework of appropriate *ninjo* (neen-joe), or "human feelings. One of the first things even the casual observer in Japan learns is that the Japanese measure, or try to measure, everything in terms of human feelings. Their traditional business system, they say, respects human feelings, while most foreign business systems do not.

In short, it has been typical in Japanese ethics and behavior to give precedence to human feelings in most situations where possible, including many occasions when objective-thinking Western businesspeople would unhesitatingly give precedence to profit considerations or other such "nonhuman" factors. Many of the aspects of business in Japan that baffle and frustrate Western businesspeople can only be understood in terms of *ninjo*.

Along with their dislike of purely logical responses to business management, the Japanese are inclined to be suspicious of anyone who is a smooth talker or who talks fast. They are especially turned off by someone who talks too much. On the other hand, being a good talker is cultivated in the United States and is prized as a major business asset. Thus when Japanese and American executives and politicians meet there is often a clash of values.

American executives who are inexperienced or insensitive to cultural differences often attempt to overcome communication problems with the Japanese by talking more than usual, repeating themselves, and often raising their voices. In the Japanese context of things, it is better to say too little than too much, even though it may take much longer to arrive at an understanding.

Chishiki
[Chee-she-kee]
Perceiving and Using Knowledge

Most of the special talents of the Japanese, along with their management systems, have been fairly well analyzed and described by both Japanese and Western authorities. But there is one aspect of the traditional Japanese way of viewing and doing things that is too subtle to be readily recognized and has so far remained hidden from virtually everyone.

In simple terms this ancient but still mostly secret Japanese recipe for success was a way of perceiving, accumulating and using *chishiki* [chee-she-kee] or knowledge that was quite different from the way that prevailed in the West. Not surprisingly, it was a cultural manifestation of which the Japanese themselves were often not fully aware because it was built into the culture.

Generally speaking Westerners are conditioned to look at information or knowledge as bits and pieces that are inclusive within themselves, and (except for scientists and a few other professionals) to expect nothing else and look no further.

THE FOUNDATIONS OF JAPANESE BEHAVIOR

Books, teachers, the news media, and the whole mass of information purveyors present the world to us in finite bits that, more likely than not, are almost always worthless in helping us understand the reality of the world around us.

Thus while we are inundated by a continuous avalanche of in formation, we do not have the experience to use it to understand what is actually going on—in education, in business, in politics, or whatever—and therefore do not benefit from it as much as we could or should.

The Japanese, on the other hand, traditionally had a different approach to viewing and using information—and approach that was often below the conscious level but was of vital importance when it came to end results. Apparently because of the influence of Shintō, Buddhist, and Confucian beliefs, the Japanese look at life and all of its facets, including knowledge, as part of a continuous flow of events, all interrelated, all essential to each other.

Unlike Westerners who still tend to seek and utilize just enough information to get by or accomplish immediate, short-range goals, Japanese treated the search for and utilization of information as an ongoing thing, without end, regardless of how or when they intended to use it. One result of this was that until the traditional Japanese way of doing business began to fail Japanese companies tended to automatically take an active rather than reactive approach to information.

While Western executives tend to wait for events to take place and then react to them, the Japanese managers tended to anticipate events, based on the flow of information coming in, and act in a way to influence or take advantage of their outcome.

Generally speaking, this very substantial difference in the way the Japanese and Westerners looked at and reacted to information had a profound effect on the ability of Japanese companies to control their destinies. It gave them the information and guidelines they needed to make continuous, minute corrections in their policies and practices, in the same way that ship navigators constantly make corrections to contend with the shifting wind and water.

However, Japan's traditional view and use of knowledge virtually ended in the 1980s when they began facing foreign competition for the first time and companies started incorporating Western practices into their business management, resulting in the companies coming down with the same narrow-minded and short-sighted practices that made Western economies so fragile.

Until the debacle of the 1980s Japanese companies, despite the image they give to outsiders, were run very much like democracies in which the power of the presidents and other high executives was limited. A significant percentage of the employees played a direct role in management's decisions.

Section chiefs in Japanese companies (the famous *kacho*), along with special teams, spent a great deal of their time researching product and project concepts and the activities of competitors and reporting on them to the higher echelons of management. The overall body of information that went into the management of Japanese companies, therefore, tended to be substantially larger, and often of a much higher quality, than what went into the management of the average Western company. This accounted for much of the strengths of traditionally run Japanese firms.

Until the traditional Japanese way of viewing and using knowledge becomes the foundation of all economic and political activity the world will continue to be handicapped by policies and practices that are irrational and harmful.

Koto to Shidai ni Wa
[Koh-to to She-die nee Wah]
Circumstantial Truth

One of the first things that early Western visitors observed about the Japanese, beginning with Townsend Harris (America's first diplomatic representative in Japan), was their apparent disregard for the truth in the "Western" sense. Harris reported that they did not know the value of a straightforward and truthful policy and that they never hesitated to utter a falsehood when the truth would have served the same purpose.

Harris was regarded by the Japanese as a dangerous enemy agent, so it should not be surprising that an attempt was made to keep him in the dark [they also provided him with a female companion in an effort to keep him occupied]. But many others who came after Harris reported the same thing, so it is important to look closely at the Japanese view and use of truth.

The truth in Japan has never been based solely on absolute principle but has been expressed more in *amae* or human terms as something that is relative and depends upon circumstances and obligations. Just as obligation and circumstance change, so does truth. A primary rule in traditional Japanese society was that nothing should be allowed to disrupt the surface serenity of existence. When the Japanese were asked a question, their natural impulse was to give an answer that would please the inquirer, even when it was not true. If they did not have a proper or plausible answer, they would answer in vague terms or give no answer at all to avoid telling a lie.

Another aspect of truth in present-day Japan has to do with personal responsibility, decision making, and group orientation. Individuals are often strictly limited in what they can say because they cannot act or pass judgments or make decisions independently. This often puts the Japanese in a position of not being able to say anything about a certain matter.

Foreign managers should be aware of this syndrome and develop tactics for getting around it when it occurs—tactics that are within the humanistic guidelines of the Japanese way but do not diminish either logic or rationality.

Jicho / Shinchō
[Jee-choh / Sheen-chohh]
Staying Out of Trouble

Another distinctive feature of Japanese life that is designed to promote *wa* and help the individual maintain essential dignity is expressed in the word *jicho* Jee-choe), which means "to respect oneself;" to be prudent. Another term for this aspect of Japanese culure is *shinchō* [sheen-chohh], which means to respect oneself and be cautious.

THE FOUNDATIONS OF JAPANESE BEHAVIOR

As is so often the case, however, respecting oneself in the Japanese context is not exactly the same as within Western cultures. Practicing *jicho* means to do nothing that would result in criticism and lessen one's chances for success. It means to be exquisitely wary of getting involved in anything that might make one stand out from the crowd and become subject to criticism. The need to avoid criticism, of course, has a profound effect on the options and behavior of employees and managers in Japanese companies.

The weaknesses of this system are obvious, and played a leading role in the inability of Japan to compete on even terms with the newly risen economic powers of Asia. Sociologists recognized the problem in the 1980s and began to call for more individual freedom and responsibility in the workplace; but for the most part, business executives did not acknowledge it until the late 1990s. However, the power of the traditional system was such that most of them could do very little about it.

When foreign managers are faced with this *jicho* syndrome they should, again, use tactics to get around it that will not add to the problem; tactics that conform to the *wa* and *amae* elements of Japanese culture.

Kao wo Tateru
[Kow oh Tah-tay-rue]
"Save My Face!"

Most "old-fashioned" Japanese executives still believe it is rude to state opinions or unpleasant truths frankly because there is the possibility of loss of face. Americans, especially, are in the habit of laying all their cards on the table, but the Japanese have been conditioned to speak vaguely and ambiguously rather than to make frank statements that might give offense.

This basic difference in attitudes and manners puts both Japanese and Westerners at a disadvantage when they are dealing with each other. Western business executives too often assume that their openness is being reciprocated, and it may be too late to rectify matters when they discover their mistake.

It is common to hear businesspeople say they will not or cannot do something because of the respect they must pay to their face or because it might scar their company's face. Still, the Japanese are always being forced to put their face on the line for one reason or another; therefore, they frequently use the phrase, *Kao wo tatette kudasai,* or "Please save my face!"

This is another area of life and work in Japan that foreigners must take into account when dealing with the Japanese. One of the culturally accepted ways to surmount this problem is to discuss it in one-on-one private meetings outside of the office—most often a dining and drinking tete-a-tete.

Tatemae / Honne
[Tah-tay-my / Hone-nay]
The Two-Faced Syndrome

The concepts of *tatemae* (tah-tay-my) and *honne* (hone-nay), also manifestations of *amae,* might be called the yin and yang of Japan. They are invariably used in tandem and play a significant role in all areas of Japanese life. *Tatemae* which figuratively means a "face" or "facade" of something is primarily used by the Japanese in reference to masking one's real thoughts or intentions. *Honne,* on the other hand, literally means "honest voice" and refers to one's real intentions.

In virtually all contexts—social, business, or political—these contrasting principles are used to cloak the truth or reality of situations that might be inconvenient or embarrassing to acknowledge publicly. This kind of behavior is, of course, common in most societies, but in Japan it has been raised to a fine art and is an institutionalized aspect of Japanese behavior that exists in all relationships. Foreign business executives, politicians, and diplomats alike who run afoul of this Japanese characteristic may never know what hit them.

In business, the *tatemae/honne* factor is perhaps used primarily to conceal some kind of failure and secondarily to camouflage intentions that might prove disadvantageous if done openly. One example of a *tatemae/honne* action is when the president sends a director of the company to take over a subsidiary ostensibly because that person is the only one capable of handling the job, while the real intention is to get rid of a potential rival.

To contend with the tendency of the Japanese to resort to the *tatemae/honne* tactic requires personal antennae that are sharply attuned to the nuances of Japanese behavior. Considerable skill in maneuvering around the ploy is also necessary if one wants to maintain a working relationship with the individual, group, or company concerned.

Ignoring the rule of *wa* that says one will maintain harmony even in the face of such deception invariably results in embarrassment (on the Japanese side), then anger (often on both sides), and finally retaliation. Japanese who fail to abide by the rules of *tatemae/ honne* behavior are likely to be ostracized.

For foreigners not attuned to the Japanese way, it is doubly difficult to discern between a *tatemae* and the even more popular Japanese penchant for leaving things ambiguous. This often entails diluting possible adverse repercussions from any source for any reason in order, for example, to avoid giving the impression of taking an inflexible stand. In this case, the only practical recourse for the inexperienced foreigner is to call in a third party who knows how to penetrate the *tatemae* facade or ambiguity screen without ruffling *wa*.

Of course the more Westernized the individual Japanese are the less likely they are to resort to either a *tatemae* or ambiguity—unless they are members of a team or group and must conform to the team mentality.

Oyabun / Kobun
[Oh-yah-boon / Koe-boon]
Living and Working in a Vertical Society

With limited exceptions, human relations in Japan, particularly the formal and professional, are based on vertical or superior-subordinate relationships. There is, of course, nothing unusual about a society based on a hierarchical arrangement of inferiors and superiors. Most, if not all, societies are founded more or less on this structure. What makes Japan's vertical society different is that traditionally there has always been a distinctive relationship between individuals and groups, or no relationship at all. It was the character of this relationship or lack of relationship that underpinned not only the etiquette and ethics of Japanese businesspeople but also most of Japanese behavior in general.

During Japan's long Feudal Age, this superior-subordinate principle was most often expressed in business contexts by the terms *oyabun* (oh-yah-boon), meaning "boss," "employer," or "master"; and *kobun* (koe-boon), which means" follower," "retainer," or "employee." Shop, factory, and restaurant owners; the heads of construction gangs; political organizations; and even criminal bosses were the *oyabun.* Their employees or followers were the *kobun. Oya* means "parent," while *ko* means "child," and is indicative of the connotation of these words.

The *oyabun-kobun* system is alive and well in Japan today, although it is not always officially described as such. In many shops, work groups, and even hoodlum gangs, the boss is still deferentially referred to as *oyabun,* and the employees and group members behave in the best *kobun* manner. Period films in which the *oyabun/kobun* system is a prime feature are perennially popular fare among Japan's movie going and TV-watching millions.

Throughout Japanese history *oyabun* was an honorable title, often with the prestige that goes with the present-day Western title of president. Westerners can win some cultural goodwill by learning how to use the title in a positive way.

Tsukiai
[T'sue-kee-aye]
Paying Social Debts

The Japanese are naturally sensitive to incurring new obligations arbitrarily because there are so many they can't avoid and because discharging their normal obligations is a heavy burden. Honoring the obligations that develop between individuals who have a special relationship—not always a happy or pleasant duty—is more often than not done simply to maintain friendly relations for the sake of *tsukiai* (t'sue-key-aye), as the Japanese so commonly say.

In practical terms, *tsukiai* refers to the social debt students owe their professors, employees owe their employers, politicians owe their patrons, or that all people owe to anyone who does them a favor, especially of a vital nature whose effects are continuous over an extended period of time. To owe *tsukiai* and to have someone owe you *tsukiai* in Japan is an important social and economic factor.

All Japanese are under strong pressure to honor their *tsukiai* debts. Failure to do so is a serious transgression if the occasion is an appropriate one, such as when a professor seeks a favor from a former student who now occupies a high position in some company or government office.

Foreign businesspeople should be especially aware of the *tsukiai* aspect of Japanese culture and use it to improve and maintain their relationships with their Japanese employees and counterparts.

Kaisha
[Kie-shah]
The Company as a Community

The Japanese word for company, *kaisha* [kie-shah], has strong connotations of "community." In referring to their place of employment, the Japanese typically add the term *uchi* (uu-chee), which means "inside" or "my house," in a possessive sense: - *uchi-no kaisha* [uu-chee-no-kie-shah] or "my company." This means a lot more than "The place where I work."

For those Japanese who work for large, well-known companies, the place where they work, *shokuba* (show-kuu-bah), generally takes precedence over their profession or the kind of work they do. When asked what they do for a living, the Japanese generally will not say they are teachers, engineers, carpenters, salespeople or whatever. They will say they are members of the staff of Chiyoda High School, of Sanyo Electric Company, of Takenaka Construction Company, or of Nissan

Motors, etc. The kind of work they do, *shokugyo* (show-kuu-g'yoe), takes a back seat to *shokuba,* the place where they work.

The extent to which the Japanese identify with their employers is so strong it often prevents them from developing close links with others in their profession. In some professions, members of different organizations do, in fact, avoid communicating with each other.

In the United States, two people in any work category can often establish a deep and satisfying rapport within minutes of their first meeting, even under the most casual *or* incidental circumstances. Such relationships can be especially deep and satisfying if the two happen to be in the same profession, whether they are truck drivers, bakers, or doctors. In Japan, such spontaneous horizontal relationships have traditionally been more or less taboo, and are still not commonplace except in formal situations such as convention meetings.

The fact that the loyalty of individual Japanese workers or managers is almost totally absorbed by their own group has traditionally made it difficult for them to establish close relationships with outsiders who were in the same line of work—a cultural factor that has become weaker with time but is still alive and well because of sensitivity about company technology and other company matters.

Another traditional business practice that seems especially strange to the foreign executive is that in Japan the most capable or hardest working employee is not always the most likely to be promoted. The seniority system notwithstanding, the rank-and-file Japanese do not approve of professionally superior people being promoted faster than they are. They are afraid the promoted person will be more concerned about himself or herself than about their fellow workers. The Japanese way has been to promote the person who gets along with everybody, is good at maintaining harmony, is flexible, and can be expected to be concerned about the welfare of all.

Recognition and advancement in Japanese companies still generally depends upon length of service with the company, age, amount of schooling, the school the employee attended, and demonstration of the right attitude. Young people who want to climb the executive ladder tend to do so by quietly building up seniority and practicing *jicho* [jee-cho], "respecting oneself." This means that they will take every precaution not to invite criticism or attract undue attention.

No doubt the key reason why the superior-subordinate ranking system in Japanese society remains powerful is because it makes all employees totally dependent on those above and below them. All members must do their part to avoid jeopardizing the entire group.

With this in mind, it is not difficult to understand why thirty-year-old employees at Mitsui & Company or Hitachi or Suzuki Electric are not about to disturb the harmony they have with their co-workers, inferiors, or superiors, since they are likely to spend their whole working life with them. The employees' contentment and success depend upon the continuing goodwill of their co-workers.

These factors play a significant role in how individual Japanese managers react to and interact with their foreign employees, their foreign counterparts in business relationships, and with foreigners who contact them with business propositions.

Ichi-ryu, Ni-ryu, San-ryu
[Ee-chee-re-yuu, Nee-re-yu, Sahn-re-yuu]
First-class, Second-class, Third-class

All of Japan's enterprises across the board are first classified according to industrial category, then by size and market share, and finally by whatever group of companies the individual firm may be affiliated with. All the larger and more important firms in each industrial category are ranked by their fellow members, as well as others, in relation to their standing when compared with all other enterprises in the same category.

A major company is called an *ichi-ryu* (ee-chee-re-yuu) or "first-class" company. A *ni-ryu* (nee-re-yuu) company is a "second-class" company; a *san-ryu* (sahn-re-yuu) is a "third-class" company. Those below third-class are seldom ranked.

The gap between first-class companies and most second-class firms is usually considerable, emphasizing that each industrial category in the country tends to be made up of a few very large firms and a large number of medium-size and small firms. The ranking of the firms in the second and third classes is not always as clear-cut as among the *ichi-ryu,* but the leading *ni-ryu* and *san-ryu* firms are very conscious of their relative ranking. They continuously strive to elevate themselves to a higher class.

Competition for the title and prestige of an *ichi-ryu* company is also intense and continuous, and is part of the motivation that spurs the Japanese economy.

Just as Japanese companies vie to achieve or maintain the highest rank, competition among young Japanese high school and college graduates to enter *ichi-ryu* companies is equally intense. Until recent years at least, working for a first-class company was more important to most Japanese than pure economic considerations, because social status was primarily determined by place of employment. Traditionally in Japan, social status took precedence over economic status, and still today the social motive often outranks the profit motive (a value many non-Japanese find hard to swallow). The prestige of working for a first-ranked company in Japan extends from the chief executive officers down to the lowest laborers, and in fact constitutes a kind of economic caste system.

Another characteristic of Japanese industry is for each of the larger firms to have a host of smaller subsidiary and affiliated subcontract *(shita-uke* [ssh-tah-uu-kay]) firms clustered around them. The subsidiary companies are known as *ko-gaisha* (koe-guy-shah) or "child-companies." There are two types of affiliated companies: *chokkei kigyo* (choke-kay-e- keeg-yoe), or "direct-line" companies, and *keiretsu kaisha* (kay-e-rate-sue kie-shah) or "aligned companies." Direct-line companies most resemble wholly owned subsidiaries.

The relationship between "aligned" companies and the larger "parent" companies is less precise and less intimate. The parent company may supply capital to the aligned company and provide various marketing functions. The degree of the alignment, ultimately, is determined by the percentage of its production that it is obligated to sell to the parent company, which in turn determines its dependence on the larger firm.

To fully understand how the Japanese economy works it is essential to know the relative rank of companies, the other companies they are affiliated with, and the kind of relationships they have. Foreigners planning on approaching Japanese companies for the first time should do this kind of homework in advance.

Shikomu
[She-koe-muu]
Training in "Company Morality"

The Japanese like to say, "The enterprise is the people." This means that a company cannot be separated from the people who make it up; that is, members of a company are bound together by emotional, economic, and social ties that transcend all others. The Japanese do not believe that employees can or will make their full contribution to the enterprise unless they are totally committed to the company and give it their highest loyalty. This is another reason why major Japanese firms prefer to hire employees directly from school, when they are young and "unspoiled" and more susceptible to being imbued with the company philosophy.

The training Japanese companies put new employees through to instill their particular philosophy is referred to as *shikomu* (she-koe-muu). This is a special kind of training that includes not only techniques but also the morality and philosophy of the actions required to accomplish a job. Master carpenters in Old Japan, for example, would send their apprentices to the theater to learn the ethics of life. When apprentices later made mistakes with the saw or hammer, the masters would upbraid them and ask if they had not yet learned anything at the theater.

The Japanese philosophy is that the company with good human relations will succeed, while the company with bad human relations will fail. The smooth functioning of human relations within companies, at least in principle, takes precedence over what the section, department, or sometimes even the whole company is supposed to accomplish.

This human-relations type of management preferred by the Japanese is based on face-to-face physical contact within groups, and with individuals in other groups with whom they have established relations. This, of course, is another aspect of the role of introductions and go-betweens. It also explains why the Japanese business system has generally precluded conducting business by telephone until face-to-face contact has been made and a basis for a substantial degree of *amae* has been established.

Some larger Japanese companies have a version of the Western custom of bringing young people in as internees. In Japan, however, the customs is known as *kenshusei* [kane-shuu-say-ee], which actually translates as "trainees," and there is a basic difference in the practice. In some of these companies the experience lasts for only one day. In other companies the sessions may be as long as 30 days. The sessions consist of listening to lectures and viewing presentations. No actual work is involved.

Foreign companies in Japan are well-advised to stick to the Western version of internees.

Shakai no Kurabu
[Shah-kie no Kuu-rah-buu]
The Company as a Social Club

Akio Morita, one of the founders of the famous Sony Corporation,* once remarked that Japanese companies look more like social organizations than business enterprises. Morita was, of course, referring not only to the junior-senior, parent-child vertical structure of Japanese companies but also to the famous paternalism of the larger ones.

To understand and work with a Japanese company, it is indeed helpful to think of it in terms of a combination of an exclusive club, a cooperative union and a business enterprise because it incorporates attributes of all three.

Japanese industry as a whole is characterized by the existence of a few huge companies that dominate each particular industrial category and are usually aligned with a *zaibatsu-like* group of other firms. Beneath these giant companies is a thicker layer of medium sized firms, some of them independent and others satellite to one of the larger enterprises. Way below these two upper layers is a mass of small to miniscule shop-factories that are often dependent on the larger firms for their day-to-day existence.

It is very important for foreign companies planning on or already doing business in Japan to be thoroughly familiar with this structure of the Japanese economy.

---

*I had a remarkable experience with Sony five years after it changed its name from Tokyo Tsushin Kogyo K.K. [Tokyo Communications Industrial Corporation] to Sony. At the time I was editor of the Tokyo-based trade journal, *The IMPORTER*. Before changing its name the company took a one-third of a page ad in the magazine [the smallest size offered] on a three-month contract [the shortest time-frame offered], promoting a small transistorized radio brand-named Sony.

The ad got Tokyo Tsushin Kogyo K.K. General Distributors in Canada and Delmonico in New York as distributors, and resulted in the company adopting the brand name Sony as its corporate name. On the 5th anniversary of the name-change the company sent us a full page ad to celebrate the occasion. The ad was full of English errors. Our publisher, Ray A. Woodside, had our Japanese office manager telephone Sony and request per-mission to correct the English. The manager who had created the ad refused. Woodside then sent me and our office manager to the Sony head office in Shinagawa to explain why it was important both to the company and to our magazine to correct the English. He not only refused our request but blacklisted *The IMPORTER*, and they never again advertised in the magazine.

Juyaka
[Juu-yah-kuu]
"Big" Executives"

As in most enterprises everywhere, there are three categories of personnel in a large Japanese company: the *jimukei* (jee-muu-kay-ee), or administrative personnel; the *gijutsu-kei* (ghee-jute-sue-kay-ee), or technical personnel; and the *ippan* (eep-pahn) or "common" staff. This is one of the few similarities between traditional Japanese companies and non-Japanese firms. For one thing, larger Japanese companies hire only university graduates for administrative positions. Examples of junior and senior high school graduates making their way up the managerial hierarchy in Japan are still rare.

There are also three levels of employees in larger Japanese companies. These are the *yaku-in* (yah-kuu-eene), or executives from director on up; the *bukacho* (buu-kah-choe), or middle and lower management made up of department and section heads and their assistants; and the *hira-shain* (he-rah-shah-eene), or employees without rank. The following table gives the administrative titles (grades) commonly found in larger Japanese companies:

Kabunushi (Kah-buu-nuu-she) / Stockholders
Torishimariyakukai (Toe-ree-she-mah-ree-yah-kuu- kie) / Board of Directors
Kaicho (Kie-choe) / Chairman of the Board
Daihyo Torishimariyaku (Die-h'yoe Toe-ree-she-mah-ree-yah-kuu) / Representative Director
Shacho (Shah-choe) / President
Senmu Torishimariyaku (Sane-muu Toe-ree-she-mah-ree-yah-kuu) / Director & Executive Vice-President
Jomu Torishimariyaku (Joe-muu Toe-ree-she-mah-ree-yah-kuu) / Director & Senior Vice President
Jonin Kansayaku (Joe-neen Kahn-sah-yah-kuu) / Standing Auditor
Bucho (Buu-choe) / Department Head
Kacho (Kah-choe) / Section Head
Kakaricho (Kah-kah-ree-choe) / Supervisor
Hira-shain (He-rah-shah-eene) / Unranked Employees

Each Japanese company usually has one or more *daihyo torishimariryaku*—directors who have power of attorney to act in the name of the company. Besides the regular *bucho* (department chiefs), companies may also have *senmon bucho* (sane-moan buu-choe), or "specialty department heads"—individuals who have been promoted to *bucho* because of their professional skill or knowledge but have no department under them. In large companies, some *bucho* may also be corporate directors.

Ka
[Kah]
People in Boxes

The basic organizational and operating unit in most large Japanese companies is a *ka* [kah] or section made up of several persons. Each section consists of a section chief *(kacho)*, usually two assistants or supervisors *(kakaricho)*, and several staff members. Several sections combined make up a department *(bu)*, headed by a department chief *(bucho)*.

The physical makeup in a section is a "box"—desks arranged to form a rectangle with the manager and his assistants at the front of the formation and the junior members strung out along the sides.

Within each of these basic boxes, responsibility and activity is more or less a team effort, with work assigned to the group as a whole. Members of each section are expected to cooperate and support one another. Older, more experienced members provide new members with the direction and help they need in a continuous on-the-job training process. The effectiveness of a particular section is strongly influenced by the morale, ambition, and talent of the whole team.

Just as individuals within the section boxes are ranked according to their seniority and title (and unofficially according to their overall attitude and effectiveness), the boxes are also ranked according to their importance within the departments they make up. The larger the number of people in a box, the more important that section is likely to be. The more sections in a department, the more important that department is.

Managers are very much aware of the rank of their sections and departments, and they are naturally concerned about being assigned to a section or department ranked below what they know their own seniority and experience deserve.

Generally, the only managers in a large Japanese company who have private offices are executive directors and up.

The organizational structure within Japanese companies is rigid and does not contribute to speedy results or innovations. To counter this handicap, Japanese companies also make use of special project teams to cope with and take advantage of new technological and management development, leading some critics of the present system to predict that these teams will eventually replace the box-sections altogether.

Day-to-day company relationships with other firms are almost always administered by one or more *ka* in conjunction with the department it belongs to. This means foreigners working with Japanese companies must deal with one or more *kacho* in the company—even though the relationship might have been initiated and approved on the highest level.

Having a good relationship with the *kacho* in charge of your account is therefore imperative.

Bu
[Buu]
Finding the Right Department

Each *bu* [buu] or department in a Japanese company is made up of several of *ka* kah] or sections. The desk of the *bucho* [boo-choh], department chief, is usually the farthest from the door, near a window if there is one, commanding a good view of all of the sections.

Most of the departments in Japanese companies are similar in name to comparable departments in Western companies. In function, however, there are some outstanding exceptions; namely, the general affairs department, or *somu bu* (soh-muu-buu), and the personnel department or *jinji bu* (jeen-jee buu).

The *somu bu* has no exact counterpart in Western firms, but it is a key department in most large Japanese enterprises. It does such things as provide liaison with customers and coordinate interdepartmental relations; handle company mail; and is responsible for the telephone switchboards, maintenance, official files and stock ledgers. Since it is the *somu bu* that provides receptionists who greet callers, most initial contacts with major Japanese companies are with this department.

The *jinji bu,* or personnel department, in a Japanese company is generally larger and much more powerful than its counterpart in a Western company. It makes practically all decisions as to who is hired, where they are initially assigned, and when and where they are rotated as part of their continuous on-the-job training. Other typical departments in larger Japanese companies:

Kokusai Bu (Koke-sie Buu) / International Department
Seizo Bu (Say-e-zoe Buu) / Production Department
Kikaku Bu (Kee-kah-kuu Buu) / Planning Department
Shizai Bu (Shee-zie Buu) / Purchasing Department
Shogai Bu (Show-guy Buu) / Public Relations Department
Keiri Bu (Kay-e-ree Buu) / Accounting Department
Eigyo Bu (Aa-e-g'yoe Buu) / Sales Department
Koho Bu (Koe-hoe Buu) / Advertising Department

Even though the names of these departments are familiar, they, like the management categories, have their own unique Japanese character. In addition to the various *bu* (departments), some large Japanese firms also have what is called the *Shacho Shitsu* (Shah-choe Sheet-sue) or "President's Room." This is a team that performs staff work for the president of the company. The functions of the *Shacho Shitsu* vary in different firms and may include secretarial work, record keeping, planning, and management information systems.

The grouping, or sectioning, in Japanese organizations has a number of serious drawbacks in the conduct of business. It can hinder and block communication, not only within the individual groups themselves but also between groups, including those in the same organization. The reason for this is that in an exclusive, tightly knit, vertically aligned group, communication is more or less limited to moving upward or downward, and in most case must go through every senior member in each level of the hierarchy. If one member is absent or chooses not to act, the communication may be short-circuited.

This vertical structure often makes horizontal communication with outsiders difficult because individual links in the structure are generally not authorized to make decisions or engage in business negotiations on their own.

Until the slowdown of the economy in the 1990s even the top executive in many companies could not act as a spokesperson for a company without first reaching a consensus of opinion among other executives and managers, regardless of the subject matter—a situation that still exists in some companies. This process of consensus naturally takes time and also incorporates the possibility that there may be no response, since it is more difficult to get five, seven, or more people to agree on anything.

This is also one of the primary reasons why it is often difficult for an outsider (a journalist, for example) to call up a Japanese company and receive any kind of official policy statement or sometimes even simple details about the company's activities.

Another disadvantage of the *sempai-kohai,* or senior-junior, grouping system is that members do not want anyone upsetting its balance or harmony in any way. This makes whistle-blowing in Japan extremely rare. In earlier times criticism of seniors, especially government officials, almost always had serious consequences even when the criticism were warrented and publicly acknowledged.

There is sometimes very little or no communication between departments on a staff level. Rivalry between sections and departments in service-type companies, such as public relations and advertising, is often especially fierce, making it difficult for the client or customer who must deal with more than one group in the company.

Further, a management system based on group loyalty and seniority makes it difficult for Japanese managers to shift from job to job or company to company, even when they have the still rare opportunity to do so. The emotions aroused when this system is ignored or breaks down—as has happened in some joint Japanese-foreign ventures in the past three decades—invariably leads to unsatisfactory if not disastrous results. Being very much aware of these dangers, topflight Japanese managers generally try to avoid being assigned to joint ventures, leaving them to second-string managers or to those who are near or already in forced retirement.

The problems involved in forming a new company with old employees in Japan are formidable. The Japanese often accept the premise that the managers first assigned to such undertakings are little more than caretakers. They typically take a long-range view, resigning themselves to wait several years for capable people to come up from the bottom in the new enterprise.

Despite its failings, however, the grouping system in Japanese business management results in motivation that is both powerful and dynamic. Like the villagers of feudal Japan who could raise their social status only by out-producing their neighbors, members of the individual groups in Japanese companies can enhance their own prestige only by increasing the effectiveness and importance of their group. This instills in each member a powerful urge not only to protect the rights and interests of the group, but also to make it stand out from competing sections.

Generally speaking, a foreign company that wants to establish a business relationship with a Japanese company must establish good relations with the appropriate *ka* and *bu*, even if they start out with an introduction to the CEO, a director or some other senior executive, because it is the *ka* and *bu* that manage the actual work of the relationship.

Shu-Shin Koyo
[Shuu-Sheen Koh-yoh]
Lifetime Employment

One of the most talked about facets of Japan's traditional family-patterned company system is lifetime employment—*shushin koyo* (shuu-sheen koe-yoe) in Japanese—which, however, has never applied to the majority of the nation's workers, and has being phased down if not out in many companies.

Although a direct descendant of feudal Japan, when peasants and artisans were attached to a particular clan by birth, the lifetime employment system did not become characteristic of large-scale modern Japanese industry until the 1950s. In the immediate postwar period, losing one's job was tantamount to being sentenced to starvation. To prevent employees from being fired or arbitrarily laid off, national federation union leaders took advantage of their new freedom and the still weak position of industry to force adoption of the lifetime employment system by the country's major enterprises.

Under the lifetime employment system, all permanent employees of larger companies and government bureaus were, in practice, hired for life. These organizations generally hired only once a year, directly from schools. Well before the end of the school year, each company and government ministry or agency decided on how many new people it wanted to bring in. They then invited students who are to graduate that year (in some cases only from certain universities) to take written and oral examinations for employment.

One company, for example, might plan on taking 200 university graduates as administrative trainees and 500 junior and senior high school graduates for placement in blue-collar work. Since permanent employment was for life, companies were careful to select candidates who had well-rounded personalities and were judged most likely to adjust to that particular company or agency's philosophy and style.

This method of employee selection is known as *Shikaku Seido* [She-kah-kuu Say-e-doe] or "Personal Qualification System." This means that new employees were selected on the basis of their education, character, personality and family background rather than any work experience or technological background.

A larger Japanese company hiring new employees, as well as firms entering into new business tie-ups, were sometimes compared to *miai kekkon* or "arranged marriages." The analogy is a good one. Both employment and joint-venture affiliations were, in principle, for life. Therefore, both parties wanted to be sure not only of the long-term intentions of the potential partner but also of the character and personality—even if there are any black sheep in the family. Thus both prospective employee and potential business partner had to undergo close scrutiny. When school graduates committed themselves the commitment was expected to be total.

Choosing employees on the basis of character qualifications was especially important to Japanese supervisors and managers because they personally could not hire, fire, or hold back promotions. They had to acquire and keep the trust, goodwill, and cooperation of their subordinates and manage by example and tact.

Besides exercising control over employee candidates by allowing only students from certain universities to take their entrance examinations, many companies in Japan depended upon well-known professors in specific universities to recommend choice candidates to them each year. Some professors, especially in the physical sciences, actually parceled out the best students from their graduating classes to top firms in their field.

While many large Japanese companies still follow this traditional practice to some extent, it is no longer as sacred as it was from the early 1950s to the 1980s. In the 1990s many corporations fired and/or laid-off hundreds to thousands of permanent employees, and began hiring non-permanent employes on short-term contracts—a move that had ramifications throughout Japanese society.

Nenko Joretsu
[Nane-koe Joe-rate-sue]
The Merit of Years

Once hired by larger companies as permanent employees university graduates are placed on the first rung of a pay/promotion escalation system that will gradually and automatically take some of them near or to the upper management level. This is the famous (or infamous) *nenko joretsu* (nane-koe-joe-ray-t'sue), "long-service rank" or seniority system, under which pay and promotions are primarily based on longevity.

Job classifications on the administrative level are usually clear enough, but specific duties of individuals in the sections [*ka*] tend to be ill-defined or not defined at all. Work is more or less assigned on a collective basis, and employees tend to work according to their abilities and inclinations. Those who are capable, diligent, and ambitious naturally do most of the work. In earlier times the lazy or incompetent ones were given tasks befitting their abilities and interests. Now they are more likely to be transferred to some less demanding responsibilities or fired.

Young management trainees are switched from one job to another every two or three years, and in larger companies they are often transferred to other offices or plants. The reason for this is to expose them to a wide range of experiences so they will be more valuable to the company as they go up the promotion ladder. Individuals are monitored and informally rated, and eventually the more capable are promoted faster than the other members of their age group. The ones promoted the fastest usually become managing directors; and one of their members generally becomes president.

During the first twelve to fifteen years of employment, the most capable junior managers accrue status instead of more pay raises and faster promotions. If they prove to be equally capable in their personal relations with others, they are the ones who are eventually singled out to reach the upper levels of the managerial hierarchy as heads of departments.

Each work-section of a Japanese company is three-layered, consisting of young, on-the-job trainees (a status that often lasts for several years); mature, experienced workers who carry most of the burden; and older employees whose productivity has fallen off due to their age.

Direct, specific orders do not set well with the members of these work-sections. Such orders leave them with the impression they are not trusted and that management has no respect for them. Even the lowest clerk or delivery boy in a company is very sensitive about being treated with respect. The Japanese say they prefer general ambiguous instructions. All that work-groups want from management are goals and direction.

Because human relations are given precedence in the Japanese management system, great importance is attached to the unity of employees within each of these groups. The primary responsibility of the senior manager in a group is not to direct the people in their work but to make adjustments among them in order to maintain harmonious relations within the group.

"What is required of ideal managers," say the Japanese, "is that they know how to adjust human relations rather than be knowledgeable about the operation of their department or the overall function of the company. In fact, people who are competent and work hard are not likely to be popular with other members of their group and as a result do not make good managers," they add.

Besides "appearing somewhat incompetent" as far as work is concerned while being skilled at preventing inter-employee friction, ideal Japanese managers have one other important trait. They are willing to shoulder all the responsibility for any mistakes or failings of their subordinates—hoping, of course, there will be no loss of face.

The efficient operation of this group system is naturally based on personal obligations and trust between the managers and their staff. Managers must make their staff obligated to them in order to keep their cooperation. This also ensures that none of them will deliberately do anything or leave anything undone that would cause the manager embarrassment. Whatever knowledge and experience are required for the group to be productive is found among the managers' subordinates if managers are weak in this area.

Like other areas of traditional Japanese management *nenko joretsu* is gradually losing out to actual competence and productivity, especially in companies that must compete with other firms in the international arena.

Sabisu
[Sah-bee-sue]
The Japanese Version of Service

Sabisu [sah-bee-sue] is the Japanese pronunciation of the English word service, but the meaning and use of the term in

Japan is quite different. It refers to far more than just providing some service, like automobile repairs, to customers, clients and other business relationships. In simple terms it refers to doing a variety of things that make the relationships very personal; that create strong emotional bonds between the two sides that live up to the obligations and responsibilities inherent in the *wa, amae* and *giri* concepts.

The ultimate standard of service in Japan grew out of the attention and level of service demanded by the shoguns, fief lords and other high-ranking individuals during Japan's long feudal age—a level of service provided by the staffs of castles and mansions as well as the thousands of inns—one day's march apart—that from the early 1600s on dotted the roads connecting Japan's towns and cities.*

---

*From 1637 on almost all of Japan's 270-plus provincial lords were required to keep their families in Yedo [Tokyo] at all times and themselves spend every other year in the capital in attendance at the Shogun's Court. They were required to march to and from Yedo with retinues based on the size and wealth of their fiefs. Maeda, lord of the largest and richest fief, was required to bring some 1,000 attendants and warriors with him on each of his journeys. This strictly enforced policy resulted in a vast chain of first-class, second-class and third-class inns being built throughout the country in 1637/8.

The system did not end until the 1850s, and was one of the defining elements in Japanese culture for over 200 years. The level of service the lords and their chief retainers demanded during their nightly stopovers during this long era gradually permeated Japanese society. Among the rules pertaining to this amazing shogunate policy: the samurai warriors of the clan-based fiefs were allowed to cut down [kill] any one along the way who did not get off of the road and bow down as the *Daimyo Gyoretsu* [Die-m'yoh G'yoh-rate-sue], or "Processions of the Lords," passed by.

This tradition of service is still characteristic of business in Japan, and is one of the reasons why living and working in Japan is so attractive to most foreigners. Foreign companies that have succeeded in Japan are invariably known for the high level of their *sabisu*.

Jimusho no Hana
[Jeem-show no Hah-nah]
"Office Flowers"

Japanese women have played primary roles in the economic infrastructure of Japan since ancient times—on farms, in shops and in the hospitality industries. Women also played a major role as factory hands in the light industries that appeared like magic between 1870 and 1880, and now make up close to 50 percent of the work force. The old view that females who worked in offices were no more than *jimusho no hana* [jeem-show- no hah-nah], or "office flowers," has gone by the wayside.

However, the world of Japanese business is still very much a male preserve. Women hold less than 15 percent of the managerial positions in the country. In the top 100 Japanese corporations less than three percent of the directors are women. But the number of women who head up their own successful companies in such areas as real estate, cosmetics, apparel, and the food business is large and growing.

Still, nearly half of all men surveyed still believe that husbands should work and women should stay at home. Many of the relationships and rituals that make up a vital part of daily business activity still closed to women. There are few women in the numerous power groups, factions, clubs, and associations that characterize big business in Japan.

But there is a female-created and managed organization that is designed to train women in their 30s and 40s for senior management positions that is having an impact. This is the *Japan Women's Innovative Network* [J-Win Executive Network] which offers a two-year training program for female executive candidates, and has some 100 member companies that support its efforts.

Foreign women who choose to do business in or with Japan face most of the same barriers that handicap Japanese women. They are not welcome or choose not to participate in the ritualistic after-work drinking and party-going that is a major part of developing and maintaining effective business relations within the Japanese system. They are generally not fully accepted as business persons first and foremost. They are generally unable to deal with other women on a managerial level in other companies simply because there generally are none.

They must also face the fact that most male Japanese executives have had no experience in dealing with female managers and have little or no protocol for doing so. Some tend to believe that women are not meant to be business managers in the first place.

This does not mean that foreign women cannot successfully engage in business in Japan, but they must understand the barriers, be able to accept them for what they are, and work around them. If they come on too strong, as women or as managers, to Japanese businessmen who are traditionally oriented, they will most likely fail. They must walk a much finer line than men.

Perhaps the most important lesson both genders of foreign businesspeople in Japan must learn is that they must go through the process of establishing emotional rapport with their Japanese counterparts. It is difficult enough for foreign men to develop this kind of relationship with Japanese businessmen, particularly when language is a problem. The challenge for foreign women who want to do business in Japan (unless they go as buyers or artists) is more formidable.

A foreign woman who is most likely to do well in the Japanese environment is one who has a genuine affinity for the language and the culture and appreciates both the opportunities and challenges offered by the situation. She must also have an outstanding sense of humor, be patient and able convince them that she is a knowledgeable, experienced, trustworthy and dependable businessperson.

What may be surprising to some is that Japanese female employees have been primary contributors to all of the most successful foreign companies in Japan. As a rule their foreign language ability and foreign culture knowledge is superior to that of males. Their dependability, common sense and practical nature make them better managers and decision-makers than most males.

All of the 100 companies that are annually ranked as the best-managed companies in Japan also have the highest percentage of female executives. As of this writing, IBM Japan has the largest number of Japanese female executives of any company in Japan. Procter & Gamble is second.

Japan's business media regularly criticizes the ongoing gender gap in Japan's workplace and states that given the fact that the population is rapidly aging and facing increasing competition from abroad it must make full use of the country's feminine resources.

Rinji Saiyo
[Reen-jee Sie-yoe]
The Outsiders

There are two categories of employees in most Japanese companies: those who are hired as permanent employees under the *shu-shin koyo* and *nenko joretsu* systems and those hired under the *rinji saiyo* or temporary appointment system. The latter may be hired by the day or by the year, but they cannot be hired on contract for more than one year at a time. They are paid at a lower scale than permanent employees and may be laid off or fired at any time.

The *rinji saiyo* system of temporary employees is, of course, a direct outgrowth of the disadvantages of a permanent employment system, which at most is viable only in a booming, continuously growing economy.

The rapid internationalization of Japan's leading corporations has also had a profound effect on their policies regarding young Japanese who have graduated from foreign universities. Until the mid-1980s most Japanese companies simply would not consider hiring someone who had been partly or wholly educated abroad. Their rationale was that such people were no longer one hundred percent Japanese and, therefore, would not fit into the training programs or the environment of Japanese companies.

Beginning in the mid-1990s Japanese corporations with large international operations began looking for a select number of young people who have been educated abroad, spoke a foreign language, and already had experience in living overseas. Ricoh Camera Company was one of the first to establish a regular policy of hiring some of its annual crop of new employees from the group of Japanese students attending American universities.

Several Japanese employment agencies also began contacting Japanese students in the U. S., providing them with information about job opportunities with Japanese companies overseas. A growing number of Japanese firms now have a policy of hiring foreigners—mostly Asians who have studied in Japan—for their international operations. These numbers remain small because Japan's corporate leaders know that foreigners, including many of those who have studied in Japan, speak Japanese well and are generally familiar with Japanese culture still do not integrate well into Japan's unique corporate cultures.

Until the Japanese themselves are able to change their cultural stripes to a much larger degree, or bite the bullet and hire a larger percentage of foreigners, Japanese companies will continue to be handicapped in competing with the likes of South Korea and China, which do not have similar cultural restraints on their thinking and behavior.

Seishin
[Say-e-sheen]
Training the Spirit

The Japanese have long associated productivity with employees having *seishin* (say-e-sheen), or "spirit," and being imbued with "Japanese morality." Company training, therefore, covered not only technical areas but also moral, philosophical, aesthetic, and political factors. Each of the larger companies has its own particular company philosophy and image, which are incorporated into its training and indoctrination programs. This is one of the prime reasons why in the past major Japanese companies preferred not to hire older, experienced outsiders; assuming that they would not wholly accept or fit into the company mold.

However, the spirit and the morality that helped make Japan the world's second largest economy until 2010 no longer provide the advantage they once did, and although they have faded noticeably, especially among younger employees, they continue to play a key role in Japanese management.

Onjo Shugi
[Own-joe Shuu-ghee]
"Mothering" Employees

The amount of loyalty, devotion, and hard work displayed by most Japanese employees is in direct proportion to the paternalism, *onjo shugi* (own-joe shuu-ghee), of the company management system. The more paternalistic the company, the harder working and the more devoted and loyal employees tend to be. Japanese-style paternalism means that the employer is totally responsible for the livelihood and well-being of all employees and must be willing to go all the way for an employee when the need arises.

The degree of paternalism in Japanese companies varies tremendously, with some of them literally practicing cradle-to-grave responsibility for employees and their families. Many managers thus spend a great deal of time participating in social events involving their staff members-births, weddings, funerals, and so on.

Fringe benefits make up a very important part of the income of most Japanese workers, and they include such things as housing or housing subsidies, transportation allowances, family allowances, child allowances, health services, free recreational facilities, educational opportunities, and retirement funds.

Japan's famous twice-a-year bonuses, *shoyo* (show-yoe), were originally regarded as a fringe benefit by employees and management, but workers and unions have long since considered them an integral part of wages. Unions prefer to call the bonuses *kimatsu teate* (kee-mot-sue tay-ah-tay), or "seasonal allowances." The bonuses, usually the equivalent of two eight months of base wages, are paid in midsummer just before *Obon* (Oh-bone), a major Buddhist festival honoring the dead and just before the end of the calendar year in December.

Foreign Employees of Japanese Companies
One aspect of Japanese management that often puzzles and frustrates Western employees is that in many Japanese companies there are no precise job descriptions. Responsibilities are generally not precisely defined, and managers do not manage by giving detailed instructions to their staffs.

The Japanese system of management is based on a team mentality that is built up over a period of time in an ongoing on-the-job training or master-apprentice approach. Young newcomers watch and listen to experienced seniors, learn the overall goals of the group, then gradually begin to pick up on and do the simplest tasks involved in the work process by imitating the more experienced group members.

Western managers may see this as a decidedly inefficient way to run a company, but the success of Japanese companies indicates that for them it works—better in many ways than the Western approach works for Westerners because of the different character of Westerners.

Factors that motivate individual Japanese to work hard and for long hours, without regard for immediate financial rewards, are primarily *wa* and *amae*-based. The identity and the sense of worth of each individual derives from membership in a viable, successful group.

Increases in income and advancement to at least the lower rungs of middle management in most Japanese companies are generally based on seniority rather than knowledge, experience, or individual effort. To be entrusted with increasingly important tasks and stay in the mainstream of advancement, individuals must constantly demonstrate their diligence and prove their loyalty to the group and to the company.

Since the group always comes first in the Japanese context, exceptionally capable people must take great care not to arouse the envy or jealousy of other group members, while at the same time daily proving their ability to work closely and harmoniously as team members.

When outstanding individuals are perceived as ignoring the team-first system, other team members generally stop cooperating with them and in the worst case scenarios ostracize them completely. Such individuals then have no choice but to request a transfer (usually to less desirable sections), quit the company, or spend their time shuffling papers without hope of advancement.

This system makes it essential that individual employees sublimate their own interests to that of the group and the company, with the result that their combined talents and energies are synergetically increased, significantly improving the performance of the group.

Another key facet of this system is that since individuals can improve their standing within the company only through team efforts, a strong competitive impulse naturally develops among the groups making up factory and office workers. Team members are encouraged to do their best, just as relay racers must support each other in order to win and share in the glory.

Because Westerners generally do not understand the nuances of Japan's team approach in company management, they tend to concentrate their communications and efforts on individuals to the exclusion of other contacts within firms. This can be fatal.

A single individual in a Japanese company usually acts as the "window" for each outside contact, but it is always important and often critical that the outsider do everything possible to keep other key people within the company in the circle of communication, in person as well as by copying them on all correspondence.

Risshin Shusse
[Rees-sheen Shuus-say]
The Japanese Success Drive

The extraordinary diligence and ambition of the Japanese is world famous. What is not so well known is exactly why the

Japanese are so success oriented. The mainspring of the seemingly frenetic drive of the Japanese—which sprang into full bloom virtually overnight when Japan's feudal Shogunate government was replaced in 1867—is apparently a combination of several historical factors. This includes their self-image as a superior people and the fact that ambition among common people was for the most part sternly suppressed from earliest times to the beginning of the modern industrial era.

During Japan's long Feudal Age (1192-1867), social class and occupations were generally hereditary. The only characteristics that were approved and rewarded were dedication to hard work and loyalty to superiors within the rigid family, clan, and Shogunate system.

With the fall of the feudal system in 1867, the, new government began an intensive campaign to bring the country up to the industrial level of the United States and the advanced European nations. Part of this campaign was an intense effort to imbue every child in the country with a concept of success known as *Risshin shusse,* (rees-sheen shus-say), or something like' 'Rise to eminence (in the world) through success!"

"*Shusse* success is distinctive in that it places major emphasis on the group instead of the individual," explains Hiroshi Hazama, professor of industrial sociology at the Tokyo University of Education. The success of the individual depends on the success of the group, beginning with the immediate work group, and by extension going all the way up to include the whole country.

Professor Hazama adds that *shusse* success is not measured in terms of wealth, but in social position. Social status is achieved by becoming a teacher, doctor, or executive. The apex of social status is to become the leader of one's group, regardless of its size, and to receive the coveted title of *cho.* This title, with its accompanying social prestige rather than conspicuous financial rewards, is the criterion of *shusse* success. Of course, the purity of this motive has suffered considerably in recent days, since contemporary life-styles in Japan make financial success an absolute necessity.

Unfortunately for Japan in the long run, the younger generations have no direct knowledge of World War II, do not suffer from any shame connected with the war, have never known poverty, and the major do not feel compelled to be slaves to work. The once honored category of being a "gung-ho employee" has lost much of its appeal.

One of the sore points among the younger generations in Japan's work force is that no matter how well-educated they are, how hard they work and how long they work it does not equate with how much they earn, so more and more of them are following the principle of doing only as much as what they perceive they are being paid for. In many cases, this means doing just enough to avoid being criticized or fired.

Katagaki
[Kah-tah-gah-kee]
The Importance of Rank

The key to Japan's superior-subordinate structured system is *katagaki* (kah-tah-gah-kee), or "ranking." All people are ranked, within whatever school they attend or organization they work for. The ranking is based on their educational background, then on their seniority, and finally on their ability to get along with others, their personality, and their talent.

In the business world, as well as in a number of the professions, the specific rank of individuals who have rank is expressed in titles that usually end in the suffix *cho* (choe), which means "chief" or "leader."

Over and above these obvious symbols of rank is the status of the company or organization in which the individual has rank. The higher ranking the employer has, the higher the status will be of any individual in the organization. This status is visually exhibited by the company or organization lapel button worn by employees of most major corporations and government bureaus.

Sempai - Kohai
[Sim-pie - Koh-hi]
Seniors and Juniors

In present-day Japan, the superior-subordinate relationship between individuals may be very conspicuous, or it may be so subtle it is difficult for an outsider to discern, much less appreciate. But it is there and is very powerful.

Today, this relationship is most often expressed in both business and educational situations by the terms *kohai* (koh-hie) or "junior," and *sempai (sim-pie)* or "senior." The word for "equal" in Japanese, *doryo* (doe-ree-oh), is seldom used because one person is usually inferior or superior to another. Equal business partnerships in Japan are, in fact, unusual because individuals who function well as equals are rare.

The basis for the *sempai-kohai* relationship has to do with education, economics, and time. It is specifically related to schools attended, year of graduation, educational level achieved, the organization one works for, longevity with the company, the size and importance of the company or organization, and the individual's title or grade.

The superior-subordinate relationship pertains specifically to individuals in the same school or same organization and those who went to the same school and work for the same organization. The status one gains from having attended a prestigious university and being employed by a leading company or government ministry carries general social status as well, not to mention the higher income it guarantees.

Individuals who graduated from X school, work for Y company, and have achieved a rank of Z in the managerial hierarchy are not obligated to behave as subordinates in any chance contact with another individual whose school or firm outranks their own. However, they will most likely do so if the other person's superior pedigree becomes known.

The education/work-based, superior-subordinate system in Japan thus touches every individual in the country one way or the other. Individuals from wealthy families are nominally inferior to their senior classmates in school and later to their senior colleagues at work. Even if their companies are family owned, they must behave in the manner prescribed for subordinates.

Kaizen
[Kie-zen]
The Continuous Improvement Concept

The genesis of Japan's now famous *kaizen* [kie-zen] or "continuous improvement" concept goes back to the introduction into Japan of Chinese arts and crafts in the 6th and 7th centuries by Korean migrants. By that time Korea had been under Chinese influence for several hundred years and during that era thousands of Koreans moved to Japan, dramatically changing Japanese culture.

Among many other concepts and practices these Korean migrants brought with them the Chinese custom of the master-apprentice system in all of their arts and crafts—an approach that had become institutionalized and sanctified early in their long history.

Over time the Korean migrants became Japanized and their master-apprentice approach was integrated into all aspects of Japanese culture. Each succeeding generation of apprentices was under pressure to equal or exceed the skill of their masters in what they designed and made, making the concept of continuous improvement an essential element in their training. The effort and time involved in the design and production of a product—the cost factor—played no role in the process.

This not only ensured a high level of quality in Japan's arts and crafts it resulted in the concept of *kaizen* becoming an integral element in everything designed and produced in Japan—everything, that is, except for the cheap foreign goods the Japanese began manufacturing in the 1870s for American importers.

Because these products were not "Japanese" and their design and quality was determined by foreign importers, they were not subject to the demands of *kaizen*. In fact, during the early decades the Japanese themselves would not buy or use the products because they were so poorly designed and cheaply made. They referred to them as *Yokohama-hin*, a derogatory term that more or less meant "Yokohama stuff," because they were shipped out of Japan from the port of Yokohama.

I first became aware of the *kaizen* concept in 1961 when I interviewed a well-known Japanese business consultant named Masaaki Imai for an article to be published in the Tokyo-based trade journal *The IMPORTER*. In 1975 Imai published a book entitled *KAIZEN – The Key to Japan's Competitive Success*, which became a bestseller.

It was not until the early 1980s that a few American executives picked up on the *kaizen* concept and began introducing it into their companies. It was not until the early 1990s that the beleaguered American automobile companies began considering the *kaizen* concept and was not until the late 1990s that they began approaching the point that they could compete with Japanese-made vehicles in quality and design.

But still today the continuous improvement concept is not an integral part of American culture. The design and quality of most products is based on keeping the production costs as low as possible. About the only Western exception to this cost and profit-first approach to designing and manufacturing products is Germany. In fact, Germans are more like the Japanese in their work ethic than any other Westerners.

In contrast to American manufacturers, American and European designers were among the first and most enthusiastic users of the *kaizen* concept, and it showed in their award-winning designs.

Gyosei Shido
[G'yoh-say-ee She-doh]
Government Guidance

Gyosei Shido [g'yoh-say-ee she-doh], "government guidance," is a feature of business in Japan that goes back to 1870 when the government took the lead in transforming the peasant-and-shopkeeper economy into a large-scale manufacturing and exporting industrial complex. Historically, the shogunate and fief governments had virtually complete control of all enterprise in Japan so this was nothing new for the Japanese.

Leadership had always stemmed from the government and authority in general, and business looked to government for guidance. These attitudes, coupled with the view of the nation as a family, allowed government to influence business, and businesses worked hard not only for their own profits but also for national well-being. There was a national consensus that Japan must be an economic power and that the duty of all Japanese was to sacrifice themselves for this national goal. Thus, the relationship between government and business was as collaborators rather than as mutually suspicious adversaries.

Gyosei shido, literally "administrative guidance," continued to play a leading role in the overall management of Japanese industries and companies up to and during World War II. Despite some significant reduction in the direct role of the government in the management of companies, introduced by the U.S.-led military forces that occupied of Japan from the fall of 1945 to the spring of 1952, the government continues to exercise substantial control over many areas of the economy.

Government controls are generally more numerous and more pervasive in Japan than in the U.S. and most European countries, so foreign companies operating in Japan must become familiar with and deal with *gyosei shido* in their category of business.

Much of the malaise that struck the Japanese economy in the late 1980s and early 1990s has been blamed on onerous government regulations and favoritism for certain industries.

The government role in business in Japan came under scathing criticism by the general population in the spring of 2011 when the Fukushima area of northwest Honshu was struck by an earthquake followed by a tsunami that literally wipe several towns and villages off the map, and wrecked a number of nuclear power plants, spreading radiation for miles around.

By that time political dysfunction in Japan had reached the level of that in the United States and several European countries, resulting in calls for fundamental changes in the role of government in business.

Amakudari
[Ah-mah-kuu-dah-ree]
Descending from Heaven

This term refers to the custom of high-level government bureaucrats retiring from agencies and ministries, usually between the age of 50 and 60, and joining companies and private organizations that are linked and/or under the jurisdiction of the government entities where they served—a custom that is common in the United States. The term literal means "descent from heaven" and refers to the descent of the Shintō gods from heaven to earth.

The ex-government officials typically collude with their former colleagues to help their new employers secure government contracts, avoid regulatory inspections and generally secure preferential treatment from the bureaucracy. *Amakudari* may also be a reward for preferential treatment provided by officials to their new employers during their term in the civil service. Some government organizations are said to be maintained for the specific purpose of hiring retired bureaucrats and paying them high salaries at taxpayers' expense.

Another custom that has long been common in Japan is for retired government bureaucats to engage in *yokosuberi* [yoe-koh-suu-bay-ree] or "side-slipping" into government corporations. Another form of this practice is known as *watari-dori* [wah-tah-ree-doe-ree], or "migratory birds," and includes former bureaucrat bigwigs becoming politicians, some of whom end up as members of the Diet.

Critics of the *amakudari* practice say it is one of the primary reasons why Japan's economic and political structure have remained impervious to needed changes over the decades. The system dates back to before World War II when many bureaucrats were sent to take over industries that had been nationalized after Japan occupied Korea and attacked China.

The system peaked in 1985, when over two percent of all the board members of major companies were ex-government bureaucrats. In the mid-1990s a series of scandals fueled growing criticism of the custom, but was not until 2002 and beyond that successive prime ministers passed legislation aimed at reducing the practice. However, in 2006 there were 27,882 such appointments to 4,576 government-connected firms that received funding from the government without having to bid against private companies for the projects. *Amakudari* and *yokosuberi* are still alive and well and are likely to be around until human nature changes.

Foreign executives in Japan should be aware that some of the Japanese companies they compete with may have a special advantage because of their ex-bureaucrat employees.

Meishi
[May-e-she]
Name Cars & When & How to Bow

Relative rank between individuals in particular enterprises and organizations and to a lesser extent between them and outsiders determines not only the behavior but also the rights, privileges, responsibilities and obligations of the individual Japanese. It is therefore very important to all Japanese businesspeople to know the rank of everyone with whom they come into contact. They must know not only their personal rank but also the ranking of their organization. One consideration here is that a section chief in a large, powerful company outranks a department head from a smaller, less important company.

This vital need to know the other's rank and employer is one of the reasons for the universal use and importance of the *meishi* (may-e-she) or "name card" in business. Cards tell about the rank of the individuals and the stature of the company they represent. [The world's first name cards were created by Chinese eunuchs who served the emperor of China and his court. Their cards were large and ornate.]

Traditionally, recipients receive business cards with both hands while bowing slightly. Now, there is less formality among those who have become more or less Westernized. But it is still important for the recipients to look closely at the name of the other person's company, its address, and the individual's title, before beginning any conversation. Besides revealing which of the two persons is subordinate to the other, they thereby establish the level of language each will use. Name cards often reveal common areas that can be quickly utilized to strengthen the new relationship—office addresses in the same area, a relative who works for the other company or a subsidiary, and other such personal links.

Foreigners doing business with the Japanese should, of course, be aware of the function and importance of name cards and know how to use them.

When meeting foreigners it is now common for most Japanese to shake hands and dispense with the bowing. Foreigner should not bow if the Japanese do not, and under ordinary circumstances there are no low bows. Low bows are used when people of low status meet someone of conspicuously high status and/or when people are apologizing abjectly for some mistake or wrong-doing.

The name-card process is naturally facilitated if one side includes Japanese translations of your name, title, and company- and, of course, if you are still using a printed version you should present your card "Japanese side up."

It is surprising how many foreign businesspeople go to Japan or greet Japanese visitors in their own offices without having Japanese-language name cards ready to pass out. It is not only a matter of courtesy. It is a reflection of your business sense, your personal image of yourself and your company, your attitude toward Japan, and more.

The latest development in meishi in Japan is a new digital version that was introduced in 2014 by a company called SanSan and began to spread across the country like wildefire. This version incudes a variety of personal and professional information about the individual, his or her employment, a printing function, likes and dislikes, and more. It will naturally go worldwide.

Ojigi
[Oh-jee-ghee]

THE FOUNDATIONS OF JAPANESE BEHAVIOR

Politeness Makes Perfect

The first-time visitor to Japan is always struck by the politeness of the people. No other Japanese trait or accomplishment has received so much praise. But there is an element of misunderstanding inherent in accepting this politeness at face value because it often misleads Westerners who are unfamiliar with the character and role of traditional Japanese etiquette.

For one thing, not all of the famous politeness of the Japanese should automatically be equated with feelings of kindness, regard, or respect for others—a reaction that is all too common for first-time visitors to Japan. The Japanese are, of course, perfectly capable of being polite in the fullest sense of the word and probably are genuinely more polite than most other people. However, what the foreigner sees, and is often overly impressed by, is strictly a mechanical role that has little or nothing to do with the personal feelings of the individuals involved.

Many Westerners, especially American tourists, have lavished praise upon the Japanese for their formal politeness. In the past most were basing their judgment of Japanese politeness on such things as the pretty elevator and escalator girls who worked in department stores and deluxe hotels. These young women, chosen for their good looks, stood and and bowed and repeated the same lines all day long in self effacing, heart-rending voices that reminded one of the chirping of baby birds that have fallen out of their nest.

The *ojigi* (oh-jee-ghee) or bow was and still is the most visible manifestation of Japan's traditional etiquette. It is used for formal greetings and farewells, when expressing appreciation or thanks, when apologizing, when asking an important favor—and when requesting any kind of action from a government bureaucrat.

Younger generations of Japanese [those born after 1960] no longer bow in casual situations, but formal situations are another matter, especially when they involve higher ranking individuals in corporations and government offices.

THE FOUNDATIONS OF JAPANESE BEHAVIOR

The occasion and the parties involved in an *ojigi* determine the kind of bow that is appropriate. The lower the bow and the longer one holds the position, the stronger is the indication of respect, gratitude, sincerity, obeisance, humility, or contriteness.

Generally speaking, there are three kinds or degrees of bowing: the informal bow, the formal bow, and the *saikeirei* (sie-kay-ee-raye) or "highest form of salutation." In the light, informal bow, the body is bent at approximately a fifteen-degree angle with the hands at the sides. This bow is used for all casual occasions between people of all rank.

The formal bow requires that the body be bent to about thirty degrees, with the hands close together, palms down, on the knees. Ordinarily the person who is bowing holds this pose for only two or three seconds, then automatically returns to the upright position. If the other party remains bowed for a longer period, it is polite for the recipient to bow again. The recipient is often the superior who will generally respond to a formal bow with a shallow bow. The other party may bow a second and a third time if the situation is important and/or serious.

The slow, deep *saikeirei* bow, which was the bow used for members of the Imperial family and Shogunate in earlier days, is only occasionally used now, generally on special occasions by older people who tend to go back to the traditional ways as they grow older.

Businessmen who go to traditional *ryokan* (rio-khan) inns or geisha houses may be greeted by maids or geisha who bow to them while sitting on the floor. It is not expected that one get down on the floor to return such bows but it can be the beginning of a lot of fun!

The main point for foreign executives to keep in mind is that they should not confuse the politeness or hospitality of the Japanese with weakness or strength on either part. If executives are really being courted by the Japanese, they may have to eventually limit the amount of hospitality they accept to avoid being put at a serious disadvantage, physically as well as psychologically. Foreigners traveling alone who go into a bargaining session with a team of Japanese after several nights on the town have their work cut out for them.

Habatsu
[Hah-baht-sue]
Behavior by the Numbers

For all of the cohesiveness and sameness exhibited by Japanese society when viewed from the outside, the Japanese are in fact splintered into thousands of big and little *habatsu* [hah-baht-sue], or groups, economically, socially, and politically. These various groups revolve around individual companies, government ministries, hospitals, schools, and sundry organizations and are of vital importance. By opening or closing doors to individuals, they hold the keys to success for the overwhelming majority.

Success, for all except the rare individual in Japan, is getting into the "right" group. Individuals can generally get into one of these choice vertically structured groups only at the bottom, when they are young and just out of school. The most conspicuous exceptions have traditionally been retiring high-level government bureaucrats. They are regularly taken into industry at executive levels because of the value of the influence they retain with their former junior colleagues in their old bureaus. This practice is commonly referred to as *amakudari* (ah-mah-kuu-dah-ree) or "descending from heaven."

One implication of the word *amakudari* is that giving up the power, prestige, security, and harmony of a vice-minister's post for the rough uncertainty of the commercial world is a considerable step-down. Another implication, of course, is that such "heavenly beings" can do extraordinary things when it comes to dealing with their old ministries.

Another, post-1970 exception to the long-established custom of bringing in new employees or group members only at the bottom is called *chuto saiyo* (chuu-toe sie-yoe), which means "mid-career appointment." Beginning about 1970, it became expedient for many companies to go outside their" closed system" to occasionally hire middle-aged, experienced personnel with needed technical expertise-thus "mid-career" recruitment.

By 2010 the custom had become common but was still considered an exceptional step.

Until the early 2000s employees in the *chuto saiyo* category were generally not treated like regular employees. Their pay was generally one or two steps below that being received by regular employees in their own age group (because to pay them the same would be "unfair" to the employees who had been with the company all their working lives). They were—and often still are—discriminated against by other employees in various subtle ways.

Despite the *amakudari* and *chuto saiyo* exceptions where major enterprises (but not government jobs) are concerned, most desirable companies are still basically closed to the entry of outsiders except by young people just out of school who come in at the bottom of the pyramid. Once people have become members of a large company or elite organization and have spent several years there it becomes either difficult or impossible for them to become fully accepted members of other organizations.

There are several reasons for this. In a system in which promotion, income, and prestige are primarily based on seniority, a new member coming in anywhere except at the bottom (or the top) breaks the chain and may throw everyone directly below the new member off schedule for life, since there are only a specific number of upper-level managerial and executive slots.

When Japanese workers quit a large company after several years and move to another one they cannot take their personal connections and good relations with them. Japanese managers who have switched employers and spent more than ten years with their new companies frequently report that they are still regarded as outsiders.

Quitting a large, well-known company and going to another one—or being transferred by a parent company to a distant subsidiary or a young joint venture company—is therefore a serious proposition for Japanese managers, because it means they have been cast adrift from the ties that mean the most to them.

Since both the grouping and advancement-by-seniority systems in Japan put everything on a personal basis, close human relations are the cement of Japanese society, in business as well as private life. It is still common for one company to refrain from doing business with another company until the managers involved in the business have developed personal relations with satisfactory *amaeru*.

This process of developing the necessary personal relations before establishing business ties with a new company is prescribed, meticulous, and time-consuming. In virtually every situation, there is some kind of *habatsu* relationship that must be dealt with.

Gakubatsu
[Gah-kuu-baht-sue]
Rule by Cliques

As in all countries, Japan's institutions of higher learning are ranked, unofficially, by age, origin, size, wealth, reputation of the staff and facilities, and their political and economic influence. Most important for the ambitious young person in Japan is that they are also ranked on the basis of the career opportunities in business and/or government that are almost completely reserved for their graduates.

In the early years of Japan's modernization, top government posts and choice managerial positions naturally went to graduates of the first universities, some of which were government sponsored. As the years passed and other universities appeared, graduates of the oldest institutions continued to monopolize the best jobs in the country simply because they were favored by their other graduates who occupied top positions in most leading government ministries and companies.

This practice was inevitably categorized under the term *gakubatsu* (gah-kuu-baht-sue) or "school cliques." While informal, these cliques, each one pertaining to the graduates of a specific, elite university, continue to dominate top posts in government and in many commercial enterprises.

Until the recession of the 1990s Tokyo University—Todai [Toe-die] for short—was the apex of Japan's educational pyramid. Hundreds of young men and women impaired their health and brought great mental suffering on themselves and their families each year in their attempts to pass the entrance examinations with a high enough score to get into Todai. Almost every year there were one or more students who committed suicide because of repeated failures to win admittance.

Japan's young people knew only too well that if they do not get into Todai they would probably be barred forever from several top-ranking companies and ministries because these institutions hired mostly Todai graduates. By the same token, those who succeeded in getting into Tokyo University knew they had it made the rest of their lives. It often seems, in fact, that it didn't make too much difference whether they learned anything or not at Todai, just as long as they got in and graduated.

Japanese universities hold entrance examinations once a year. If students fail, they have to wait a full year before trying to get into the same university again. Some high school graduates who fail to get into the universityof their choice wait until the following year to try again rather than take the examinations to a less desirable university. They are popularly called *ronin* (roe-neen), which literally means "wave men," the old term for samurai warriors who lost their clan lord and roamed the country, often causing trouble.

A similar situation exists, to a lesser degree, for several universities ranked immediately below Todai, such as Keio (Kay-oh), Waseda (Wah-say-dah), Kyoto University, Hitotsubashi (He-tote-sue-bah-she) and Kobe University. Like Todai, they enjoy the special patronage of certain enterprises and government bureaus.

However, by the first decade of the 21st century the mystique of Todai had undergoing a metamorphosis—a phenomenon that was welcomed by most Japanese. Its dominance of several of the leading ministries of the government and the upper echelons of management in many of the country's ranking companies continues, but there is increasing criticism of both the arrogance and the incompetence of Todai graduates, particularly in regard to the growth and profit positions of some of the companies they head. .

One Todai professor summed up the situation by saying that Todai graduates were intelligent but lacked imagination and the innovative spirit that was needed by Japanese industry today. He described the typical graduate as a "superior mediocrity." This criticism has resulted in efforts to upgrade the Todai approach to teaching and in the attitude of its graduates, refurbishing the tainted image of the famed university.

A special word refers to the' 'job-getting success" of graduates of specific high schools and universities: *shushokuritsu* (shuu-show-kuu-reet-sue). This means "the rate of employed versus the number of graduates." The percentage of graduates from a particular school who succeed in getting jobs with desirable companies or government ministries determines the school's *shushokuritsu—the* "job-getting success" of its students.

Sports activities are very popular and important in Japanese universities because leading companies like to hire well-known athletes. There is usually a club for each sport. Among club members, the *sempai-kohai* (senior-junior) syndrome reigns supreme, with emphasis on proper behavior of juniors toward seniors-behavior based on complete subordination. A graduate *sempai* who is particularly outstanding for some reason is often referred to as *dai-sempai* or "great senior."

Occasionally, a *dai-sempai* who is a graduate of a particular university and is in a responsible position in a prestigious company will accept an invitation from his old sports club to visit its summer training camp. There, both school and club ties are reaffirmed, and it is made explicit that such graduates will do all they can to help members of the club get into their companies after graduation.

Such relationships, established on a hot summer day on the playing field, are cherished for a lifetime by students who end up being employed by the companies concerned, and they serve as a significant factor in major personnel decisions by leading Japanese companies.

Many of the elite universities set certain standards, such as the number of A's individuals earn during their senior year, to determine whether or not students get a recommendation from their professors to a desirable company.

University students in their senior year also compete for the privilege of doing their theses under the direction of the most popular professors, who are often retained as consultants by leading enterprises and therefore have strong connections with the personnel departments of these companies. Each professor conducts a "thesis seminar" for fifteen to twenty students, helping them select topics and guiding them in their research and writing.

Western executives serving in Japan who are recognized authorities in certain business fields might benefit themselves and their firms by offering to act as free advisers to these "thesis seminars."

By establishing such a relationship with universities, with individual professors and graduating students, the executives would come into contact with outstanding young men and women looking for career opportunities.

Nenbatsu
[Nane-baht-sue]
Up by the Year

Besides the *gakubatsu* or "school clique" factor in the headier heights of Japan's business and professional world, there are also *nenbatsu* or "year clubs" in some ministries and major corporations. A "year club" is a grouping of all the new university graduates who entered the company or ministry the same year regardless of what university they graduated from.

As members of a particular year club accrue seniority in their organization, they look out for each other. Their entry-year loyalty may be so strong that they avoid developing close relationships with other co-workers, including those from the same university but from different graduating classes. Members of the same year club expect to be promoted at the same time and thus move up the executive ladder together. Even when new employees do not formally align themselves in such clubs, they still form a close bond and they expect to go up in unison.

Some Japanese critics blame the year clubs and advancement by seniority for an excess of assistant managers and managers in a typical Japanese company. But the larger and older the company, the deeper the systems are likely to be entrenched. The trend in the past has been for new companies and rapidly growing smaller companies to start out with a merit system, or at least a partial merit system, for pay and promotion purposes. But in many cases the passing of time has seen the gradual appearance of the seniority system. The Japanese, say the country's businessmen-philosophers, like the security of it.

Success in Japan has traditionally been tied to educational level as well as to the prestige of the university attended. Therefore, the highest ranking universities have been more or less sanctified as a result of their exalted role in the nation's life. This situation provides the foreigner with a way to get partially inside Japanese society. I say' 'partially" because no foreigner has ever entered all the way inside Japanese society and is not likely to in the foreseeable future.

The best way for foreigners to get into Japanese society is to attend and graduate from one of the better-known and respected Japanese universities. The ties with Japanese classmates approximate those among themselves, and foreigners are also accorded a certain amount of respect and acceptance by Japanese who graduated before or after them. Attending school together in Japan is very much like becoming a blood brother in the Native American sense.

Shokaijo
[Show-kie-joe]
The All-Important Introduction

In Japan a *shokaijo* [show-kai-joe], or introduction, derives its power from the practical and psychological need of the Japanese to have some kind of guarantee before they can bring themselves to become involved with someone with whom they do not have an *amae* relationship.

Westerners are familiar with the practice of giving and receiving introductions in the regular conduct of their businesses. But the system used in the United States, for example, does not compare with the role the *shokaijo* play in Japan. Americans are not compelled by generations of conditioning and centuries of tradition to treat an introduction as anything more than mere politeness. American businesspeople on the receiving end of a *shokaijo* can turn callers away or decline to take any action on their behalf without fearing that the relationship with the person who gave the introduction will suffer. Not so the Japanese, particularly if the introduction is from a valued friend, a superior, or an important business contact. Businesspeople who are most susceptible to an introduction are those most concerned with maintaining "face" among those to whom they owed *tsukiai*.

The *shokaijo* itself is institutionalized in Japan with wide ramifications that touch on many aspects of daily life. It owes its role and power to several cultural influences: the exclusivity and wariness toward outsiders that is inherent in the vertically structured group system, the desire of the Japanese not to lose face for any reason, the principle of group responsibility, and their tendency to avoid personal involvement with outsiders or strangers.

The least that can be said is that in Japan it has long been considered rude to approach a person or a company directly without an introduction from a mutual friend or business contact. If you go through proper channels—that is, the *shokaijo*—some of the responsibility shifts to the third party and provides an element of security. Many Japanese continue to be suspicious of anyone who approaches them without an introduction, and most Japanese would not think of making such an approach themselves in dealing with other Japanese.

There are several types of *shokaijo* commonly used by the Japanese when they want to meet someone for business purposes. The most common one is from someone to whom the person you want to meet is personally obligated, such as a superior, an old university professor, someone who has helped the family, or a close relative or personal friend. Another popular type of introduction is one from a senior executive in a company with which the person you want to meet has substantial business obligations. This might be, for example, the vice-president of the bank where that person has made a loan or from some important buyer or supplier.

Less effective but still useful is an introduction from a senior officer in a company with which the individual's company has business relations. A non-personal introduction from a well-known bank, company, or other organization is probably the weakest of the introductions but is better than none. Foreign executives who plan to do business in Japan or are already in business there certainly should make an effort to obtain introductions to any individual or company they want to approach.

While the best introduction is often a personal one to an individual, foreign businesspeople will generally find that they cannot rely *only* on an approach to a single individual in a Japanese company. To be successful, any approach must also take into consideration all other sections and departments concerned.

However, while there is only one "right" way to meet a Japanese businessperson in the Japanese context of things, which is through an introduction, the Japanese regularly make exceptions to this where foreigners are concerned. In fact, foreigners who show up at Japanese companies without having either appointments or introductions may be shown into the office of the highest executive available. This, however, is usually no more than Japanese politeness and cannot be taken as a sign of interest in the callers or their purpose.

Knowing that the *shokaijo* system exists and knowing how to use it leads many individuals in Japan to specialize in taking unethical or unappreciated advantage of it. Some people make a business of "selling" their status by giving introductions to persons and accepting gifts and other favors in return. In particular, advertising-space salespeople are notorious for taking advantage of the power of the *shokaijo*. These salespeople somehow get closer to business executives or well-known, respected and influential figures—the higher and the more important the better—and ask them to write a few words of introduction on several of their name cards. The introduction usually consists of only a few words, like "This is Mr./Ms. So-and-So. Please do what you can for him/ her. "

The salespeople then take the cards to the business executive's circle of friends in other companies and sell advertising space to them. There is often little or no talk about advertising as such. The salespeople are more likely to say that their publication would like to have the "support" of the company. By this time the executive on the other end of the *shokaijo* knows exactly what is going on and, more often than not, will sign the advertising contract or in some cases hand over the amount of money suggested by the salesperson. Most companies in Japan have a special fund set aside, called *tsukiai-ryo,* or "social debt funds," to payoff such debts.

It should be emphasized, however, that businesspeople who are put in a position in which they feel obligated to payout *tsukiai-ryo* may consider that they are being "taken" and may resent it strongly.

Hoshonin
[Hoe-show-neen]
The Important Role Guarantors

Besides the *shokaijo* itself the need for guarantees led to the development of another institutionalized function and figure in Japanese society, namely, *the hoshonin* [hoe-show-neen] or "guarantor."

Over the centuries the importance of personal-based relationships and maintaining *wa, amae* and *tsukiai* resulted in the development of the institutionalized practice of individuals bringing in *hoshonin* [hoh-show-neen] or "guarantors" to back up their sincerity and actions when beginning the process of creating new relationships with other individuals and/or companies.

The presence of a *hoshonin* was generally required by the individuals or companies being approached when they did not know the person or company approaching them. The reason for this caution was simple. The obligations involved in personal and business relationships were typically demanding and if any discord or problem developed repercussions could be serious.

Both individuals and companies were and still are exceptionally sensitive about their reputation—about the possibility of the lost of face—and often require third-parties to guarantee the behavior of new contacts.

In numerous instances involving official documents, such as establishing credit, the Japanese system requires a *hoshonin* who accepts responsibility for the individual's character, trustworthiness, and behavior. In business and professional matters the person who introduces someone to another becomes partly and sometimes wholly responsible for whatever may come of it—both the good and the bad. A *hoshonin* may be expected to accept full responsibility both in principle and in fact.

There are, of course, cases of an introduction from one Japanese to another apparently having no more significance than the somewhat casual letter or note of introduction common in the West, in which nothing more complicated or compelling than simple courtesy is involved. But favors that are small and completely insignificant from the Western viewpoint are not bestowed lightly in Japan, especially when they occur through an introduction.

Foreigners wanting to make new business or professional contacts in Japan should obtain *shokaijo*, introductions, from individuals or institutions well-known and/or important to the other party—and in effect serve as *hoshonin*. They should also take advantage of the power of *hoshonin* to help open doors and smooth relationships.

Chukai-Sha
[Chuu-kie-Shah]
The Go-Between

The ultimate in the *shokaijo* concept in Japan is the *chukai-sha* (chuu-kie-shah), or a person who acts as a go-between in business affairs. Of course, the concept and role of the go-between or intermediary is familiar in the West. The Japanese, however, have institutionalized the function to a greater extent—the *chukai-sha* in business, like the *nakodo* (nah-koe-doe) in arranged marriages, plays a much greater and more important role in Japanese life.

The advantages of using a *chukai-sha* in business are numerous and not really mysterious. In the first place, the better go-betweens have a wide circle of friends and connections and are respected and trusted individuals. In Japan, where face-to-face communication by strangers is very difficult, the go-between can carry on most of the dialogue, help each side avoid losing face, and eventually smooth the way for the development of a formal relationship between the two parties if their interests merge.

The *chukai-sha* can be especially helpful to the foreign businessperson in Japan, providing invaluable counsel on what to do and what not to do to maintain peace and harmony and negotiate successfully with Japanese companies. Recognizing this, some foreign companies operating in Japan have had *chukai-sha* on retainer for years.

Finding an appropriate go-between is not that difficult. They are generally known to chambers of commerce, business associations, banks, government ministries from which they have retired, and companies they have worked with.

Kyōsō
[K'yohh-sohh]
Competition by the Numbers

Before the modern era in Japan, most personal competition, especially within groups, was taboo because it resulted in friction and disharmony—the opposite of *wa*. In fact, the Japanese were taught that competition for personal, selfish purposes was criminal. The Japanese did not have a word for competition—*kyōsō* [k'yohh-sohh]—until it was deliberately coined by educator Yukichi Fukuzawa, the founder of Keio University, in the 1880s.

While there are now many areas and ways in which the Japanese compete against each other fiercely, especially in education, the Japanese business system in general has maintained the old sanctions against individual competition, and it continues to promote the concept and practice of group action and team spirit.

There are other cultural factors involved in the taboos against personal competition among the Japanese. One of the worst things that can befall any Japanese is to be shamed and made to lose face. Personal competition, with a few sanctioned exceptions such as in athletic contests, always carries with it the danger of being shamed. Foreign business executives should always remember that their contacts in Japanese companies, regardless of their rank, are not "officially" in competition with their colleagues, and the Japanese will resist any attitude or behavior that might make them appear to be competing against their own co-workers.

There have been and still are numerous occasions when the foreign business executive says, in effect, to a Japanese contact, "Look! You cooperate with me and help me get this deal through, and it will make you a big shot in your company!" The one thing that would inevitably make it impossible for the Japanese to reach the higher or highest echelons of their company would be for them to break step with their co-workers or to strike out on their own.

Even though the Japanese are imbued with a compulsion to better themselves, to rise to the same level as those who are higher, and even though this compulsion is one of the prime forces motivating the Japanese economy, the extraordinary drive this gives the Japanese must generally be channeled into group effort within the framework of the Japanese company system.

Ringi Seido

[Reen-ghee Say-ee-doe]
Putting It in Writing

In addition to the cooperative-work approach based on all employees contributing according to their abilities and inclinations, many large Japanese companies divide and diversify management responsibility by an old system known as *ringi seido* (reen-ghee say-ee-doe), which generally means "written proposal system." This is a process by which lower level managers [kacho and bucho] play key roles in management decisions by coming up with written proposals that are passed up the chain-of-command...giving birth to the "bottoms-up" management associated with many Japanese companies.

Briefly, the *ringi* system consists of proposals written by staff members of sections or departments that are circulated horizontally and vertically to all layers of management for approval. Managers show approval of the proposal by stamping the document with their *hanko* (hahn-koe) name seals in the prescribed place. Managers who disapprove pass the document on without stamping it or put their seal on it sideways or upside down to indicate conditional approval. In some new companies signatures instead of name seals may be used.

When approval is not unanimous, higher executives may send the document back with recommendations that more staff work be done on it or that the opinions of those who disapprove be taken into consideration. Managers may attach comments to the proposal if they wish.

In practice, workers who originate a *ringi-sho* or "written proposal document," informally consult with other managers before submitting it for official scrutiny. They may work for weeks or months to get the idea approved unofficially. If they run into resistance, they will invariably seek help from colleagues who owe favors. They in turn will approach others who are obligated to them.

The efficiency and effectiveness of the *ringi seido* varies with the company. In some it is little more than a formality, and there is pressure from the top to eliminate the system altogether. In other companies the system reigns supreme, and there is strong opposition to any talk of eliminating it. The system is so deeply entrenched in both the traditional management philosophy of the Japanese and the aspirations and ambitions of younger managers that it will probably be around for a long time.

Foreigners negotiating with Japanese companies' should be aware that their proposals may be the subject of one or more *ringi sho* This not only takes up a great deal of time (they must be circulated in the proper chain-of-status order), but also exposes them to the scrutiny of as many as a dozen or more individuals whose interests and attitudes may differ.

Whether or not a *ringi* proposal is approved by the president is primarily determined by who has approved it by the time it arrives. If all or most of the more important 'managers concerned have stamped the *ringi-sho,* chances are the president will also approve it.

While this system is cumbersome and slow, it generally helps build and maintain a cooperative spirit within companies. In addition, it assures that when a policy change or new program is initiated, it will have the support of the majority of managers.

As can be seen from the still widespread use of the *ringi seido,* top managers in many Japanese companies are not always planners and decision makers. Their main function is to see that the company operates smoothly and efficiently as a team; to see that new managers are nurtured within the system, and to pass judgment on proposals made by junior managers.

Nemawashi
[Nay-mah-wah-she]
Behind the Scenes Lobbying

Just as originators of a *ringi* proposal will generally not submit it until they are fairly sure it will be received favorably, Japanese managers in general do not, unlike their foreign counterparts, hold formal meetings to discuss subjects and make decisions. They meet to agree formally on what has already been decided in informal discussions behind the scenes.

These informal discussions are called *nemawashi* (nay-mah-wah-she),"spinning or revolving the roots of a plant or tree," to help make sure it will grow when planted.

Nemawashi protocol does not require that all managers who might be concerned be consulted. But agreement must always be obtained from the right person-meaning the individual in the department, division or upper echelon of the company management who really exercises power.

If you do not have an introduction to a high-level contact in a Japanese company one of the best things you can do is identify the *kacho* [kah-choe], section chiefs, in the area or category of business concerned, and make the initial informal contact through them. If detailed talks with one or more *kacho* go well they in turn can identify and introduce the appropriate *bucho* [buu-choe], [department heads].

Even if you do have a high-level contact in a company you must still get the willing cooperation of the *kacho* and *bucho* concerned before your project will get off of the ground floor. If the high-level contact you have is impressed with you and your project he or she will make the necessary introductions.

Kaigi
[Kie-ghee]
Meeting to Talk

Since business management in Japan is more of a consensus process, Japanese managers probably have twice as many meetings, *kaigi* (kie-ghee), as their counterparts in the West. Some standard meetings:

Tori Shimariyaku Kai (Toe-ree She-mah-ree-yah-kuu Kie) / Board of Directors Meeting
Juyaku Kai (Juu-yah-kuu Kie) / Directors Meeting
Bucho Kai (Buu-choe Kie) / Department Heads Meeting
I-in Kai (Ee-een Kie) / Committee Meetings

Hishokan
[He-show-kahn]
Where are all the Secretaries?

As most Western executives would readily admit, they simply could not get along without their female secretaries. In many ways, secretaries are as important, if not more so, than the executives themselves. In Japan only the rare executive has a female secretary whose role approximates the function of the Western secretary.

The reason for the scarcity of secretaries in Japan is manyfold. The collective work groups, decision making by consensus, face-to-face communication and the role of the manager as harmony-keeper instead of director practically precludes the secretarial function. Another factor is the language itself and the different language levels demanded by the superior-subordinate system, plus the fact Japanese does not lend itself to dictation.

The closest the typical Japanese company comes to having secretaries in the American sense are receptionists—usually young women who are stationed at desks in building lobbies and in central floor and hall areas. They announce visitors who arrive with appointments and try to direct people who come in on business without specific appointments to the right section or department. When callers who have never had any business with the company and have no appointment appear at one of the reception desks, the receptionist usually tries to line them up with someone in the General Affairs *(Somu Bu)* Department.

Small Japanese companies and many departments in larger companies do not have receptionists. In such cases, no specific individual is responsible for greeting and taking care of callers. The desks nearest the door are usually occupied by the lowest ranking members in the department, and it is usually up to the callers to get the attention of one of them and make their business known.

Keiyaku
[Kay-e-yah-kuu]
The Japanese Contract

Japanese executives generally do all they can to avoid getting involved with the law and the courts. In the past, it was customary in Japan for both parties in a dispute to be regarded as equally guilty. Justice was often both harsh and expensive, and under any circumstances it was usually wise to avoid bringing oneself to the attention of the authorities.

In Japan today the law is still regarded as a costly and complicated process. The foreign tendency to bring lawyers in on business negotiations and to draw up minutely detailed *keiyaku* [kay-ee-yah-kuu], contracts, can be still upsetting to the Japanese. They prefer general agreements that allow the parties to discuss and negotiate particular points as they come up, leaving both sides a great deal more flexibility.

The Japanese executive's credo is that every effort should be made to avoid problems by cooperating on an individual and personal as well as company and industry level. When problems do arise, they should be solved by arbitration and compromise. Their view is that since it is impossible to know exactly what is going to happen in the future, detailed, written contracts are bound to become outdated in just a short time.

In the past, there were few written contracts in Japan. They depended instead on *yakusoku* (yah-kuu-so-kuu), "verbal agreements," with the parties bound to each other by goodwill and obligation. When such agreements were reached and were of some importance, they were usually marked by a drinking party and the ceremonial clapping of hands for a prescribed number of times in a particular cadence.

While disliking and distrusting written contracts, Japanese executives recognize that they have little or no choice but to use them in their international business. They are especially sensitive to the fact that they usually do not know their foreign counterparts very well, cannot *amaeru* with them in full confidence and trust, and cannot depend on dealing with the same individuals from one day to the next, much less from year to year.

The Japanese concept of contracts makes it imperative that the two sides stay in close contact with each other, communicating in detail about all of the large and small points that come up in cross-cultural relationships. These points should be in written form first, then discussed face-to-face, and then summarized in writing.

A significant part of the Japanese image of contracts is that circumstances are bound to change so contracts should be flexible enough to account for these changes. They also tend to presume upon the *amae* element of their relationship with other companies that allows them to alter their actions on their own when circumstances change without unduly upsetting the other party—a prerogative that is seen as reciprocal.

Sekininsha
[Say-kee-neen-shah]
Finding Where the Buck Stops

In Western countries there is almost always one person who has final authority and responsibility, and it is easy to identify this person. All you have to do is ask, "Who is in charge?" Generally speaking, in Japanese companies no single individual is in full charge. Authority and responsibility are dispersed among the managers as a group.

The larger the company, the more people are involved. When there are mistakes or failures, Japanese management does not try to single out any individual to blame. They try to focus on the cause of the failing in an effort to find out why it happened. In this way, the employee who made the mistake does not lose face, and all concerned have an opportunity to learn a lesson.

Highly placed Japanese executives advise that it is difficult to determine who has real authority and who makes final decisions in a Japanese company. "Even a top executive must consult his colleagues before he makes a decision because he has become a high executive more by his seniority than his leadership ability. To keep harmony in his company he must act as a member of a family," said a Sony director.

In approaching a Japanese company about a business matter, it is therefore almost always necessary to meet and talk with the heads of several sections and departments on different occasions. After having gone through this procedure, you may still not get a clear-cut response from anyone, particularly if the various managers you approached have not come to a favorable consensus among themselves. It is often left up to you to synthesize the individual responses you receive and draw your own conclusions.

It is always important and often absolutely essential that outsiders (foreign or Japanese) starting a new business relationship with a Japanese company establish good rapport with each level of management in the company. Only by doing so can outsiders be sure that their side of the story and their needs and expectations will get across to all the necessary management levels.

Earle Okumura, a consultant and one of the few Americans who is bilingual and bicultural and has had extensive business experience in Japan, suggests the following approach to establishing lines of communication with a Japanese company when the project concerns the introduction of new technology to be used by the Japanese firm:

Step 1 - Ask a director or the head of the Research & Development Department to introduce you to the *kacho* (section chief) who is going to be directly in charge of your project within the department. Take the time to develop a personal relationship with the *kacho* (such as eating and drinking with him or her) then ask them to tell you exactly what you should do, and how you should go about trying to achieve and maintain the best possible working relationship with the company.

Step 2 - Ask the R&D *kacho,* with whom you now have at least the beginning of an *amae* relationship, to introduce you to the counterparts in the Production Department, Quality Control, and Sales Departments, etc., and go through the same get-acquainted process with each of them, telling them about yourself, your company, and your responsibilities. In all of these contacts, care must be taken not to pose any kind of threat or embarrassment to the different section managers.

Step 3 - After you have established a good, working relationship with the various *kacho* concerned, thoroughly explained your side of the project, and gained an understanding of their thinking, responsibilities, and capabilities, the third step is to get an appointment with the managing director or president of the company for a relaxed, casual conversation about policies, how much you appreciate being able to work with the company, and the advantages that should accrue to both parties as a result of the relationship.

Do not, Okumura cautions, get involved in trying to pursue details of the project with managing directors or presidents. They will most likely not be familiar with them and, in any event, will be more concerned about your reliability, sincerity, and ability to deal with the company.

Before foreign business executives commit themselves to doing business with another company, they check out the company's assets, technology, and financial stability. Japanese executives are first interested in the character and quality of the people in the other company and secondarily interested in its facilities and finances. The Japanese put more stock in goodwill and the quality of interpersonal relationships in their business dealings than most Western executives do.

O'Miyage
[Oh-Me-yah-gay]
Giving to the Cause

Another important aspect of maintaining good relations, keeping *wa,* and getting things done in Japan comes under the general heading of gift-giving. There are, broadly speaking, three categories of gift giving in Japan. On the lowest order are the *te-miyage* (tay-me-yah-gay) or "hand gifts" given to the host when you are invited to someone's home or to someone who does you a favor while you are traveling. Gifts given when making home visits are likely to consist of cakes, pastries, boxes of fruit, or traditional Japanese food delicacies. It is, however, not the custom for the host to open these gifts while the guest is present.

The second category of gifts is of those given in midsummer and at the end of the year. The midsummer gift-giving occasion is called *Chugen* (chuu-gain); the year-end gift-giving season is known as *Seibo* (say-e-boe). The end of the year is the most important gift-giving season in Japan, because this is when virtually all companies give gifts to their clients and customers.

Companies, in fact, are the biggest gift-givers in Japan. They give year-end gifts to "reward" customers for past patronage, to express gratitude, and to build up obligations for future business. During the years that I had monthly printing done by Dai-Nippon (die-neep-pone), Japan's largest printing company, the department in charge of my account had a case of beer or some other useful commodity delivered to my home every year just before New Year's. Being one of the largest printing companies in the world, with thousands of customers, one can imagine the size of Dai-Nippon's annual year-end gift bill.

On an individual basis, subordinates give gifts to superiors, and people in general present gifts to *onjin* (own-jeen) or "benefactors" to whom they are obligated for past favors.

Most Japanese business executives who go abroad take gifts of varying value to give to people they meet. For casual gifts to people who show them some hospitality, the visitors usually give relatively inexpensive gifts that are representative of Japan, such as folding fans, carved *kokeshi* (koe-kay-she) dolls, or miniature calculators. For important, established, or potential business associates, the gifts are often fairly expensive and elaborate.

Because such gift-giving is institutionalized, the Japanese are naturally pleased when their foreign guests or business counterparts follow the custom. A set of golf clubs or a case of good Scotch is probably more appreciated in Japan than in any other country.

The third category of gift-giving in Japan comes under the heading of *0'tsukaimono* (oh-t' sue-kie-moe-no), "something to be used," and is practiced throughout the year on every social and economic level. An *0'tsukaimono* gift is specifically given to a person from whom you are seeking a favor. Rather than regard the gift as a form of bribery, the Japanese feel that it is rude to ask a favor of someone without giving them something in return.

Gift-giving on an elaborate scale is not a recent development in Japan. Like so many other things, it has its roots deep in the culture, and in earlier times it was as meticulously hedged in by rules as other areas of Japanese life. There were, in fact, specific rules prescribing exactly what item was appropriate to give to people on particular occasions and according to their social rank.

It was also prescribed as to how such gifts should be wrapped, using what materials in what manner. And finally, the procedure for presenting gifts to important superior-ranking persons was minutely detailed. The importance attached to the proper choice, wrapping, and presentation of gifts is apparent from the fact that well-to-do families often had one member whose primary responsibility was to know and advise the household on gift-giving protocol.

Moshiwake Arimasen
[Moe-she-wah-kay Ah-ree-mah-sin]
Apology without End

With so many areas of life so meticulously prescribed, it was virtually impossible for the Japanese of feudal Japan to avoid transgressions against their highly refined and aggressively enforced etiquette system. To compensate for the bonds their manners imposed on them, and to help prevent the system from breaking down under its own weight, the Japanese gave great power to the apology. Most minor and many major transgressions against the system could be wiped clean by admission of guilt, an apology, and a demonstration of humility and regret.

An apologetic, humble attitude, especially by public figures, is still considered an essential virtue by the Japanese. In fact, for the Japanese to function smoothly within the web of their social obligations, it is necessary to learn very early how and when to humiliate themselves and to apologize humbly. There are so many ways in which the Japanese can give or take offense that the apology is also an institutionalized practice. The Japanese apologize for real as well as "pretended" shortcomings as often as Americans brag about their imagined ability and learning. The purpose of the Japanese apology is to avoid ill-will, friction or anything else that might rub supersensitive people the wrong way.

The apology expressed by the term *sumimasen* (sue-me-mah-sin)—literally, "it [the guilt I feel] is without end"—is one of the most common word for saying "I'm sorry" where small transgressions are concerned. It is also used as "thank you," to express thanks for small routine favors. A very common informal term for very minor transgressions, such as bumping into someone lightly, is *gomen* [go-mane]. If you want to be more formal, the full term is *gomen nasai* [go-mane nah-sie], please excuse me.

Moshiwake arimasen (Moe-she-wah-kay ah-ree-mah-sin)—"I have no excuse" (and submit myself to your mercy)—is used in more serious situations. These terms, expressed several times amidst bowing and facial signs of humility and regret, may be followed by *O'yurushi kudasai* (Oh-yuu-rue-she kuu-dah-sie), "Please forgive me."

Within the context of the Japanese morality, the greatest sin is to be guilty of any crime and refuse to admit or express regret over it. Thus, exceptional importance is attached to the apology.

For a Japanese (also for Koreans and Chinese) to confess to a minor transgression, apologize, and express sincere regret is more or less the same in the Western sense as a guilty person being punished and rehabilitated at the same time. If the admission and apology are sincere, the Japanese generally forgive completely, rather than demand some kind of punishment as is the case in the West.

Inseki Jinin
[Een-say-kee Jee-neen]
The Japanese Cop-Out

There is substantial historical evidence that people steeped in the religions and philosophies of Asia have tended to conduct themselves on the basis of changeable circumstances rather than basic truths or unchanging laws, with the result that they had different values and behaved differently than their Western counterparts in their personal, business, and political relationships.

Rather than basing their attitudes, customs, and laws on universal principles, the Japanese developed an exquisitely precise system of doing things based on form and process—a system that came to be known as *doh* or "way." There was literally a prescribed way for doing everything, and conforming to this *doh* was the official, sanctioned morality.

Thus it happened that a highly stylized way of doing things often took precedence over what Westerners regard as human rights and other high-minded concepts generally labeled as ethics or principles—and frequently over common sense as well.

Japan's traditional bend-with-the-wind morality was an efficient social and political system when the country was isolated from the rest of the world, but it has since been a mixed blessing on the international scene. On the one hand, it gives the Japanese a conspicuous advantage in being able to design their behavior to suit the circumstances. On the other hand, it regularly leads to friction between them and their foreign counterparts and competitors.

One of the most conspicuous examples of the flexibility of Japan's ethical system is the custom known as *inseki jinin* (een-say-kee jee-neen), which can be translated into English as something like "take responsibility and resign." It refers to the practice of politicians, businesspeople, and others assuming responsibility for accidents, scandals, and various forms of unethical or illegal behavior, resigning from their positions and thereby absolving their organizations-and other individuals in their organizations of any blame for wrongdoing.

Historically, the custom of *inseki jinin* was a means for those in power—and sometimes the public-at-large—to force miscreants of one kind or another out of positions they abused without resorting to violence and unduly upsetting the harmony of the whole. It was also occasionally resorted to by high-minded people who did, in fact, remove themselves from office because of genuine remorse over the actions of others, with the aim of bringing moral pressure on them to alter their behavior.

With few exceptions, however, the standards applying to acts of *inseki jinin* were based on policies and not principles, with fairness, equality, and justice taking a backseat to expediency and perpetuation of the system.

The long-sanctified custom of *inseki jinin* is more common in Japan today than it was before the establishment of a legal system based on universal principles. Now thousands of companies, professional organizations, and branches of the government can, and often do, take advantage of *inseki jinin* to avoid full responsibility for unprincipled behavior simply by a public show of sacrificing their figurehead leaders.

Those who believe in and practice *inseki jinin* say they are taking moral responsibility for disturbing society. It is not an admission of guilt, but recognition that public harmony was disturbed. It is not intended to eliminate the behavior that resulted in the disturbance but is designed to restore harmony.

There may be occasions when the *inseki jinin* system is a fair and humane way of resolving situations, but generally it is an autocratic way of condoning unprincipled behavior, usually at the expense of the public or less privileged people.

Scandals in the 1990s and again in 2010 resulted in a wide spectrum of Japanese people publicly criticizing the evils of the *inseki jinin* system, pointing out that it was one of the greatest obstacles to improving the morality of business and politics in the country. But the fact that the *inseki jinin* syndrome continues to play a key role in both business and politics in Japan today, despite the growing chorus of protests, demonstrates clearly that expediency still takes precedence over principles within the Japanese establishment.

One of the primary reasons for the strength and survival of the *inseki jinin* system is that it has traditionally been complemented by the power of the apology in Japanese culture. As in the rest of the Confucian sphere of Asia, the Japanese people ritualized, sanctified, and institutionalized the concept and use of the apology. Like confession in the Catholic Church, an apology in Japan has long been accepted as ablution of all minor sins and at least partial atonement for more serious transgressions as well.

In the Japanese context of things, failure or refusal to apologize for wrongdoing is regarded as virtually as bad, if not worse, than the deed itself. The Japanese tend to look upon such behavior as the epitome of arrogance and are infuriated by it. Because of the importance of the apology in Japanese life, people are constantly apologizing to each other, even for the most casual things. As noted earlier, one of the most commonly used words for "thank you" [*sumimasen* / sue-me-mah-sin] also means "I'm sorry," and it is up to the listener to decide which way to take it.

As a result of this overuse and misuse of the apology in Japan, it is often nothing more than a hollow ritual. Like *inseki jinin,* it is also systematically used as a tactic to muffle criticism and divert any pressure to change.

Japanese corporations and the government are under growing pressure to create codes of ethics that would eliminate the arbitrary self-serving nature of their public and private actions. But since business and political behavior in Japan are a direct reflection of the traditional core culture, there is no way such behavior can be changed without deeper and more fundamental changes in the culture.

Mizu Shobai
[Me-zoo Show-bye]
The "Water Business"

Mizu shobai (me-zoo-show-bye), literally "water business," is a euphemism for the hundreds of thousands of bars, cabarets, night clubs, "soap houses" (formerly known as Turkish baths... Turks finally complained because of the sexual implications of the label), hot spring spas, and geisha inns that flourish in Japan. The term *mizu* is applied to this area of Japanese life because, like pleasure, water sparkles and soothes, then goes down the drain or evaporates into the air (and the business of catering to fleshly pleasures was traditionally associated with hot baths).

Shobai or "business" is a very appropriate word, because the *mizu shobai* is one of the biggest businesses in Japan, employing several million men and women.

Drinking and enjoying the companionship of attractive young women in *mizu shobai* establishments is an important part of the lives of Japanese businessmen. There are basically two reasons for their regular drinking. First, ritualistic drinking developed into an integral part of religious life in ancient times; from there it was carried over into social and business life.

Thus, for centuries, no formal function or business dealing of any kind has been complete without a *uchiage* (uu-chee-ah-gay) drinking party to mark the occasion. At such times, drinking is more of a duty than anything else. Only a person who cannot drink because of some physical condition or illness is normally excused.

The second reason for the volume of customary drinking that goes on in Japan is related to the distinctive superior-subordinate relationships between people and to the minutely prescribed etiquette that prevents the Japanese from being completely informal and frank with each other *except when drinking*.

Because the Japanese must be so circumspect in their behavior at all normal times, they believe it is impossible to really get to know people without drinking with them. Sober people, they say, will always hold back and not reveal their true character. They feel ill at ease with anyone who refuses to drink with them at a party or outing. They feel that refusing to drink indicates a person is arrogant, excessively proud, and unfriendly. The ultimate expression of goodwill, trust, and humility is to drink to drunkenness with your co-workers and with close or important business associates in general. Those who choose for any reason not to go all the way must simulate drunkenness in order to fulfill the requirements of the custom.

Enjoying the companionship of pretty, young women has long been a universal prerogative of successful men everywhere. In Japan it often goes further than that. It has traditionally been used as an inducement to engage in business as well as to seal bargains, probably because it is regarded as the most intimate activity men can share.

Many Westerners find it difficult to join in wholeheartedly at the round of parties typically held for them by their Japanese hosts, especially if it is nothing more than a drinking party at a bar or cabaret. Westerners have been conditioned to intersperse their drinking with jokes, boasting, and long-winded opinions-supposedly rational-on religion, politics, business, or what-have-you.

Japanese businessmen, on the other hand, do not go to bars or clubs at night to have serious discussions. They go there to relax emotionally and physically—to let it all hang out. They joke, laugh, sing, dance, and make short, rapid-fire comments about work, their superiors, personal problems, and so on; but they do not have long, deep discussions.

When the otherwise reserved and carefully controlled Japanese businessman does relax in a bar, cabaret, or at a drinking party, he often acts—from a Western viewpoint—like a high school kid in his "cups" for the first time.

Many Japanese businessmen, particularly those in lower and middle management, drink often as a business relationship requirement, and generally develop the capacity to drink and keep up their day-to-day work. Since they drink to loosen up and enjoy themselves, to be hospitable and to get to know their drinking partners, they are suspicious of anyone who drinks and remains formal and sober. They call this "killing the *sake,*" with the added connotation that it also kills the pleasure.

During a boisterous drinking bout in which they often sing and dance and trade risqué banter with hostesses or geisha, Japanese businessmen often sober up just long enough to have an important business exchange with a guest or colleague and then go back to the fun and games.

Foreign executives should be very cautious about trying to keep up with their Japanese hosts at such drinking rituals. It has been all too common to see visiting executives being returned to their hotels well after midnight, sodden drunk. The key to this important ceremony is to drink moderately and simulate a modest level of drunkenness.

The economic melt-down that began in the late 1980s dramatically reduced the amount of money Japanese managers spent in geisha houses, the great cabarets, the bars, and the "in" restaurants in Japan's major cities. But like so many other aspects of Japanese life, the *mizu shobai* is deeply embedded in the overall socio-economic system, as well as in the national psyche. It is not about to disappear in the foreseeable future.

Most of the money spent in the *mizu shobai* comes from the so-called *sha-yo zoku* (shah-yoe-zoe-kuu), "expense-account tribe"—the large number of salespeople, managers, and executives who are authorized to entertain clients, prospects, and guests at company expense. Japanese companies are permitted a substantial tax write-off for entertainment expenses to begin with, and most go way beyond the legal limit (based on their capital), according to both official and unofficial sources.

It is no longer essential for foreign businesspeople in Japan to match the Japanese in their use of the *mizu shobai* in making and maintaining business relationships. But a judicious use of it can make the difference between success and failure.

Bo Nen Kai
[Boh Nane Kie]
Meeting to Forget

Japan's personally oriented management system, with its strict rules requiring workers to repress their individualism in the interest of group harmony, naturally results in friction and the buildup of stress. There are two popular annual activities partly aimed at helping to relieve the personal antagonisms that develop among group and company members: the *Bo Nen Kai* (Boe Nane Kie), "Forget the Old Year Party," and the *Shin Nen Kai* (Sheen Nane Kie), "New Year Party."

The theme of the traditional end-of-the-year *Bo Nen Kai* party, held at the place of work and marked by food and drinks, is to have a good time with co-workers and forgive and forget all the bad things that happened during the course of the year. There is no set date for the "Forget the Old Year Party." Some companies hold them several days before the last working day of the year.

New Year's, *Osho Gatsu* (Oh-show Got-sue), is Japan's most important holiday. Almost everyone is off work for three or four days, and some companies close for longer periods. The occasion is used for family and shrine visits. In most offices and companies on the first day after the New Year's break, there is an informal open-house-type *Shin Nen Kai,* or "New Year Meeting." The purpose of the meeting is for workers and managers to formally greet one another and ask for goodwill, cooperation, and help for another year. The idea is to start each new year on a positive note so as to contribute to both morale and productivity the rest of the year. Usually little or no work is done on this day.

It is also customary at this time of the year for company representatives to visit their banks and for suppliers to visit companies that buy from them.* The callers first greet their contacts with, *Akemashite Shin Nen O'medeto Gozaimasu* (Ah-kay-mahssh-tay Sheen Nane Oh-may-day-toe Go-zie-mahss)—"Congratulations on the Opening of the New Year" or "Happy New Year!"

This is immediately followed by the set expression: *Saku nen chu wa taihen Osewa ni narimashita. Mata kon nen mo yoroshiku o'negai itashimasu* (Sah-kuu nane chuu wah tie-hane Oh-say-wah nee nah-ree-mah-ssh-tah. Mah-tah kone nane moe yoe-row-she-kuu oh-nay-guy ee-tah-she-mahss). This means, loosely, "We are deeply obligated to you for your patronage and help last year and extend our deepest gratitude. We ask that you please continue doing business with us this year."

---

*Japanese businesspeople are generally more deeply obligated to their banks than their foreign counterparts. Many banks also own substantial equity in anywhere from a few to dozens of companies.

Rikutsu-poi
[Ree-kute-sue-poy]

THE FOUNDATIONS OF JAPANESE BEHAVIOR

Beware of being too Logical

As said, the Japanese business system works less on cold objectivity and logic and more on feelings. In many confrontations, the appeal that usually wins in the end is the emotional one—for harmony, for face, and for the future benefit of the majority. Emotion is the glue that binds the Japanese system together. If you want to get along with, influence, or lead Japanese employees, associates, or clients, see to their emotional needs first. Not surprisingly, the Japanese regard most Americans as *rikutsu-poi* (ree-kute-sue-poy)—too logical, too objective, too uncaring about the emotional (human) content in business relations.

Western businesspeople should keep in mind that the first and often primary reaction of most Japanese to any subject is often emotional, then ethnic, then nationalistic and then logical. It is therefore essential that any approach to them be tailored to bypass or get through this conditioned response. This is particularly important when the topic at hand has political implications.

Foreign politicians who have gone to Tokyo and made what they feel are rational, reasonable, and practical dissertations on Japan's invisible trade barriers, pointing out example after example, have been stopped cold when a ranking Japanese journalist got up and said something like, "Senator, what we really want to hear is what you think about the Japanese people!"

Put on the spot, stunned politicians had no choice but to say they admire the Japanese and think they are a superior people. The journalists then go on to write that foreign businesspeople have trouble getting into the Japanese market because they are not willing to do things the Japanese way, not because of any barriers blocking their entry.

The Japanese maintain that the problem is one of perception. They say the market appears closed because foreigners do not understand the Japanese way of doing business and do not make sufficient effort to learn. Thus when Japanese and foreign politicians meet to discuss economic problems, they are generally on different wavelengths and talk about different things.

One of the ways to get around the Japanese tendency to view everything on an ethnic and emotional basis is to acknowledge the emotional, personal factors at the outset. Give them sufficient due so that the Japanese can relate to you as an understanding and caring human being, and then get down to logical and practical concerns.

Wa/Sa
[Wah / Sah]
Harmony vs. I'd Rather not Say

First meetings between Japanese and Western executives are generally the epitome of graciousness, goodwill and enthusiasm. Westerners are often so impressed with the formal, stylized etiquette of the Japanese and the impression they give of vulnerable sincerity and desire to cooperate that the foreigners are lulled into a false sense of enthusiastic optimism.

On their part, the Japanese are generally not deliberately attempting to be disingenuous. They are simply behaving in what for them is a traditional way of greeting and getting acquainted with other people.

Situations therefore repeatedly develop in which the Western side is reacting abnormally to the Japanese, which in turn encourages the Japanese to continue behaving in a way that compounds the problem caused by both sides misreading each other's signals.

The variations in behavior derive from what author, management consultant and debate enthusiast Michihiro Matsumoto refers to as the *why/because* approach used by Westerners in communicating when it comes into conflict with the traditional Japanese approach. Matsumoto, author of *The Unspoken Way: Haragei—Silence in Japanese Business and Society* and over one hundred other books and one of Japan's best-known simultaneous interpreters, has written and lectured extensively on why the Japanese do so poorly in trying to communicate with Westerners.

He points out (in terms that are often jarringly offensive to Japanese sensibilities) that the Japanese have had no experience in using the West's *why/because* form of discourse, and generally speaking do not approve of it because their own way teaches a philosophy and ethic that is just the opposite.

Honest Western debates and negotiations are an intellectual contest in which the weapons are facts and logic. Successful debating or negotiating Western style requires precise knowledge, a rational mind, frankness, respect for other people, and good verbal skills.

Japanese repudiation of direct, frank, comprehensive communication has traditionally been so deep that being a skilled speaker was regarded as an indication of insincerity; as characteristic of someone who could not be trusted and therefore did not make a good confidant or business partner.

Although substantially weaker than in earlier times, this attitude remains a significant factor in Japan today, even in politics, as former prime ministers who were outstanding public speakers, found to their chagrin.

One aspect of this factor that regularly trips up Western executives in Japan is that they not only talk conspicuously well. They talk too much for Japanese tastes and often end up doing themselves more harm than good simply because they do not know about the Japanese distaste for effusive dissertations.

Americans, in particular, cannot stand verbal vacuums. When the Japanese side sits back quietly, makes no comments, and asks no questions, American executives too often feel they have not succeeded in making their point—a fear that all too often is true—and rush in with a new torrent of words that generally just further muddies the water.

In addition to avoiding public friction, Japan's *wa* way incorporates the idea of preventing any single individual from being held personally responsible for the success or failure of a project by spreading responsibility among the whole group.

If one side of the Japanese cultural coin can be called the *wa* way, the other side can certainly be called the *sa* (sah) way. *Sa* has a number of rather indistinct meanings, such as "well," "could be," "I'd rather not say," "who knows," and so on.

Sa is commonly used when people do not want to respond to a question or situation and want to leave their position vague. It is often something like shrugging one's shoulders or making a non-committal gesture with the hands.

The combination of *wa/sa* gives a pretty accurate idea of the rules that have traditionally governed Japanese attitudes and behavior. *Wa* gave birth to *sa* because the sanctions for disrupting harmony were very serious. The only practical approach was to keep a low profile, remain non-committal, and stay on the fence until you knew where everyone else was going.

Virtually all Western communication is couched in terms of *why/because* and is designed to get to the heart of a matter quickly, without allowing for any subterfuge. Until Japanese business leaders, bureaucrats, and politicians learn how to react to and use this form of speech, and Westerners become more sensitive to the *wa/sa* factor, there is no way to totally eliminate the misunderstandings and friction that occur when Japanese and Westerners attempt to communicate with each other.

Fortunately for both sides, the more Westernized the Japanese are the less bound they are by the demands of *wa* and the more likely they are to respond positively to the why/because approach to dialogue.

O'Machigae
[Oh-Mah-chee-guy]
A Mistake Westerners Make

Many foreign companies with operations in Japan handicap themselves by switching their personnel every two, three, or four years. In the normal course of business in Japan, it takes from two to five years before the Japanese begin to feel that they really know their foreign employer, supplier, client, or colleague.

It also generally takes foreigners transferred to Japan from one to three years to learn enough to really become effective in their job. Shortly afterward, they may be transferred, recalled to the head office, fired, or replaced by someone else. This is almost always a big mistake—an *O'machigae* [O'mah-chee-guy] in Japanese.

American executives in particular tend to pay too little attention to the disruption caused by the turnover of foreign personnel in their Japan offices. This may occur because they think more in terms of the position or slot being filled by a body that has whatever qualifications the job calls for in the United States. Generally speaking, they play down the personality and character of the person filling the position and often do not adequately concern themselves with the role that human relations play in business in Japan.

This, of course, is just the opposite of the Japanese way of doing things, and it accounts for a great deal of the friction that develops between Japanese and Westerners in business.

San
[Sahn]
The San Conundrum

The age-old custom of the Japanese to attach that honorific "san" to the first and/or last names of the people they address or refer to is one aspect of Japanese etiquette that may seem piddling to some foreigners but it can be confusing and/or upsetting to those dealing with the Japanese.

San translates as Mr. Mrs. or Miss, depending on the individual being addressed or referred to. The custom is so ingrained in Japanese culture that it sometimes appears to have lost its original intent—that is to show respect. But not using it can definitely be interpreted as disrespectful if the individual being addressed is not a junior, a family member or a friend and if the situation is formal.

Some foreigners in Japan ask their Japanese co-workers and friends to dispense with *san* when addressing them. Some foreigners, particularly Americans, ask their co-workers with whom they are on more or less equal footing to use their first names. Some Japanese may do so in informal settings, but many will add *san* to the individual's first name because they don't feel right not doing it.

To be safe, foreign managers in Japan should use *san* when addressing older Japanese employees, particularly those in managerial positions. The one time when it is common for Japanese men to drop the *san* and refer to people by their last names is during after-hours drinking sessions. It is customary for men to drop virtually all etiquette when they are drunk—and when feigning drunkenness.

Foreigners who adopt this practice when out drinking with their Japanese co-workers should do so only after the party gets loud and the Japanese have let their hair down and it all appears to be done in good fun.

To be on safe ground, foreign employers and managers who have Japanese in their foreign offices or factories should use *san* when addressing older employees and those on a managerial level. A common exception to this rule is when the Japanese concerned specifically ask that they be addressed by their first name or nickname.

Not using *san* is a degree of familiarity and intimacy that has become old hat to younger Japanese among themselves in informal situations, but once they enter the adult world the pressure on them to conform cannot be ignored.

Foreigners should keep in mind that addressing Japanese who are not Westernized without using *san* may be taken as disrespectful of the Japanese and their culture.

Dekoboko
[Deh-koe-boe-koe]
Doing Business on a Uneven Field

The view of many foreigners that Japan is a tilted playing field has two dimensions. The first dimension is more or less a genuine reflection of the business environment. The second dimension is something like a mirage that results from a combination of ignorance and the linear glasses Westerners generally wear when they look at Japan.

Unfortunately, the problems caused by this uneven field cannot be quickly resolved. No amount of goodwill or legislation by Japan—which so far has not been that forthcoming—or a clearer perspective on the foreign side, can suddenly alter the deeply rooted attitudes and practices that are responsible for the uneven character of the marketplace.

This leaves foreign executives with only one practical choice and that is to deal more effectively with the Japanese market and competition in their own home markets by learning how to maintain their balance on uneven ground. In order for foreign business leaders to keep their balance on this permanently askew field, it is first all necessary that they be able to interpret correctly, in cross-cultural language, what they see and hear.

And the problem begins, of course, with the fact that what they see and hear is often not what they get. For an accurate understanding of what is going on, they must know what such words as equality and fair mean to the Japanese.

There is a word in Japanese for equality [byōdō] but it is seldom used. In the Japanese context of things, true equality virtually never exists outside of physics. In business and political associations, as in just about everything else in Japanese life, there are inferiors and superiors.

Equality in any Japanese business relationship is therefore a situational thing that has to be interpreted in Japanese cultural terms, not according to abstract Western principles. In the Japanese system, it is automatically assumed that whatever party is stronger, smarter and/or cleverer is more equal than the other and will take more of the benefits.

Neither the "good Samaritan" principle nor looking out for the underdog were ever officially promoted or accepted parts of the historical experience of the Japanese. In the early years failure by the Western side to recognize this aspect of joint ventures with Japanese companies contributed significantly to the tendency of such relationships to come apart at the seams in a matter of a few years.

Of course, the virtual inevitability of rifts developing in joint Japanese-foreign enterprises also grows out of a fundamental difference in goals. Generally speaking, the Japanese side wants new technology, new products, and larger market share for its own growth and profitability and goes into these relationships with the intention of using the foreign partner. Fairness, *kōhei na* [kohh-hay-e nah], seldom enters the picture.

THE FOUNDATIONS OF JAPANESE BEHAVIOR

All too often, foreign businesspeople go into joint ventures with Japanese companies because they offer the easiest and cheapest way out. They either do not perceive or ignore the fact that such joint ventures often do not make good business sense, especially on a long-term basis. And when things go sour, they usually blame the Japanese side.

The concept of fairness in Western-Japanese dealings probably causes more misunderstandings and grief than any other factor. In the Western sense fairness is an abstract principle that is thought of as something universal that can and should be applied to all relationships.

In fact, it often seems that fairness is the only ethical standard Westerners have, and particularly so in the case of Americans. We tend to construct our whole world on this principle. The theme of virtually every American presentation whether a proposal or a protest is fairness whether or not we live up to the ideal.

That is all very well and good if you are dealing with people who are also fair-minded. But fairness in the Western sense is a new and still unnatural concept in Japan [and in China!], and Americans have not yet learned how to adjust to this situation.

The overall political and economic systems in Japan still function on the basis of conditional ethics and expedient policies, and both give priority to maximum benefits for the group/entity concerned.

The Japanese meltdown in the early 1990s and sudden arrival of China on the international scene changed the situation fundamentally. Almost overnight American companies shifted their outsourcing from Japan to China, with its manufacturing capacity some ten times larger than that of Japan.

The playing field for American companies in Japan is now more or less level, but newcomers to the field must do their homework if they are going to succeed. The Japanese still demand more quality and better service that Americans do.

China is a different matter. The Chinese are smarter, cleverer, more ambitious and more immune to outside criticism than the Japanese. And the United States has not learned the basic economic lesson that if the bulk of the goods sold in the country are made abroad our manufacturing base will continue to shrivel up.

And there is another factor. Japan cares very much about the continued survival of the United States as a friendly bastion of power. China does not.

Mono-no-Aware
[Moe-no no Ah-wah-ray]
Aesthetics in Business

The Japanese, like most Asians, were traditionally as concerned with emotional and spiritual things as they were with material things. This attitude led to the development of a culture in which aesthetics often took precedence over practical things. Natural beauty and things made of basic materials in a natural way became objects of worship. Communing with nature through poetry and various aesthetic appreciation cults were intimate parts of every person's life.

Takeo Doi, Japan's *amae* guru, says the Japanese preoccupation with aesthetics throughout their history was caused by their urge to *amaeru* with nature. Thus the practices involving flowers, the moon, snow, and even the sounds of insects are, in Dio's view, direct manifestations of the *amae* factor in Japanese culture.

As usual, there are several key words in Japanese that pertain to the role of aesthetics and communion with nature in Japan. One is *mono-no-aware* (moe-no-no-ah-wah-ray), which refers to an extraordinary sensitivity to nature, to beauty, and the ability to merge one's identity with that of an object or mood, especially one that is tinged with recognition of the impermanence of all things.

Another, more commonly used word is *shibui* (she-buu-ee), which refers to beauty that is in perfect harmony with nature and has a tranquil effect upon the viewer.* Then there is *sabi* (sah-bee), an attribute of beauty sometimes called "the rust of the ages" referring to moss on a rock or tree, wrinkles on the face of an aged man or woman, waste wood bleached gray by the weather. *Wabi* (wah-bee) denotes another aspect of beauty in the Japanese lexicon. It refers to materials that are the epitome of simplicity and austerity. *Yugen* (yuu-gain), "mystery" or "subtlety," connotes a type of beauty dear to the Japanese that "lies modestly beneath the surface of things."

There are more such descriptive words, all providing additional insights into the extraordinary role of aestheticism in the distinctive life-style developed by the Japanese. All are aimed at achieving a deep, satisfying sense of identity with nature—and now giving the Japanese a significant advantage in product design and packaging.

At the same time, beauty was not all tranquil harmony to the Japanese. There was another side of aesthetics expressed in the term *iki* (ee-kee), which suggests wit, flair, stylishness, and sophistication. *Iki* beauty refers to objects as well as character, habits, and personality of the individual. The person with *iki* is cool and smooth and floats through life with savoir faire.

The tradition of communing with nature through practices elevated to the level of aesthetic cults has considerably waned among the young generations in Japan. However, enough of it remains that some aesthetic appreciation and artistic skill is considered essential to the complete individual.

On the business side, many companies offer employees free classes in aesthetic pursuits such as flower arranging, dancing, and the tea ceremony. The older and more successful executives are, the more they tend to concern themselves with spiritual and emotional contentment obtained through either artistic or aesthetic activities. They may look down on, or at least feel sorry for, the executive who is too busy or too insensitive to do likewise.

Foreigners who are serious about getting to know and establishing a lasting rapport with their Japanese counterparts are well advised to also cultivate an appreciation for simple beauty and the myriad workings of nature.

---

*For a definitive discourse on aesthetics in Japanese culture see my *ELEMENTS OF JAPANESE DESIGN – Understanding and*

PART 3
Matome
[Mah-toe-may]
Summing Up

The Nihonjin Ron Factor
Despite the changes that have occurred in Japanese culture since the 1950s the deeply embedded Japanese belief that they are unique in the world because of their culture remains true to degrees that vary with the individuals and their background.

This ongoing belief is embodied in what is referred to as *Nihonjin Ron [Nee-hone-jeen Rone],* which translates as "Japanese Theory"—and refers to the unique elements in the Japanese mindset and behavior.

Studies and writings on the *Nihonjin Ron* factor have been a major industry in Japan since shortly after the arrival of large numbers of foreigners—particularly Westerners—in the late 16th and early 17th centuries when the Japanese became acutely aware that their attitudes and behavior were very different from that of foreigners.

Despite dramatic changes in the mindset and behavior of the Japanese since the end of World War II in 1945, particularly those born after 1960, there are basic differences in the way the Japanese think and act, and the subject of *Nihonjin Ron* remains alive and well in present-day Japan.

Of course, cultural differences are not unique to the Japanese. All nationalities have their own cultural values that in many cases are unique to them. This is particularly true of mainstream Americans who are the least sensitive to other cultures and typically behave in the American way without thinking about it when encountering and dealing with other people.

Cultural differences remain responsible for virtually all of the misunderstanding and friction that arises in the business relationships of Japanese and foreigners—and are particularly evident in presentations and negotiations, and among foreign employees of Japanese companies.

Mainstream Americans are more likely to clash with Japanese etiquette and ethics than any other people. These differences are especially revealed in virtually every presentation and negotiation the two sides engage in.

Americans are open and frank and are programmed to do things fast. Japanese are guarded and conditioned to do things slowly and meticulously. American executives can make decisions on their own volition; Generally Japanese executives cannot. Americans typically ask questions during presentations; generally Japanese do not. The Japanese want and need extensive, detailed material in writing that can be pored over and studied later. Americans like flashy graphics; the Japanese do not because they leave so much out.

Despite the fact that more and more Japanese corporations are hiring foreign employees for lower and middle-level jobs in Japan there is always an underlying feeling among Japanese managers that foreign employees are temporary; they will leave the company whenever it suits them, and as a result they do not treat them the same way they treat Japanese employees.

This results in many of the foreign employees assuming that the Japanese side is interested only in their special knowledge and skills and is not committed to their lifelong welfare... including those who are, in fact, dedicated employees who want to be treated like their Japanese coworkers.

This phenomenon generally pertains mostly to foreign employees of Japanese companies *in* Japan—not those overseas. Japanese managers of overseas operations typically send top foreign managers to Japan for periods of training and indoctrination in the Japanese way, but in the U.S. in particular they usually stop short of trying to Japanize their employees.

However, in countries where the Japanese feel culturally superior to the local people indoctrination and training of local employees in the Japanese way is much stronger.

Cases in which foreign executives have been appointed to top positions in Japanese companies remain rare, and are generally limited to those companies that have become international conglomerates and depend on foreign markets for a major percentage of their sales.

In many cases these changes are more cosmetic than real because of another factor in the mindset of the Japanese. There has traditionally been a dichotomy in the Japanese reaction to Westerners. On the one hand they have automatically felt superior to Westerners because their etiquette and work ethics were far more detailed, precise and sophisticated, and they were more spiritual in their beliefs and behavior. On the other hand they have traditionally felt inferior to Westerners because of the West's industrial and financial power.

This led the Japanese to be far more susceptible to change—that they knew the needed but could not accomplish on their own—if the change was recommended and promoted by Westerners who were not bound by the Japanese need for consensus among themselves, and could ignore this need. The voice of the foreigner became "the voice of the crane" in the Japanese context—the powerful, respected outsider.

There have been numerous examples of this phenomenon in Japanese history—from retired emperors and shoguns, former prime ministers, yakuza gang leaders, and other powerful individuals who controlled events from behind the scenes.

Also on the plus side, Westerners with extensive international business experience bring an element to Japanese management that is often sorely lacking.

Given the strength and staying power of the traditional Japanese way further significant changes in business management will be generational and mostly involve new technology. As long as key areas of Japanese behavior as whole remain based on traditional concepts, Westerners and other outsiders must know a great deal about the origin and essence of their morality to deal with them responsibly and effectively.

Innovation and Japan

Despite the conservative and ethnocentric stance of most Japanese the country has a growing number of entrepreneurs. During the economic slowdown of the 1990s the number of young Japanese who chose entrepreneurship rather than continue trying to find jobs in companies literally exploded. They have not become well-known outside of Japan because of little or no attention by the mainstream news media.

The list of Japanese inventors and innovators is as long and as impressive in some categories as that of Americans. These categories include electronics, biology, medicine, new materials, plastics, robotics and software.

One of the most important examples of made-in-Japan software is the Ruby programming language created by Yukihiro Matsumoto, which quickly became the most-used program for building advanced cloud applications and for changing how applications are developed for linking innovations in virtually ever industry.

Humanism plus Authoritarianism

Broadly speaking, Japan's traditional management philosophy is based on a subtle balance of humanism mixed with authoritarianism and is patterned after the Japanese adaptation of an ideal Confucian family. In Confucian ethics, the ideal family is one that follows the Five Principles: filial piety, fidelity, obedience, kindness, and loyalty to one's superior.

When the Japanese imported Confucianism from China, they switched the order of the Five Principles, making loyalty to one's superior paramount so the principles would fit more readily with their own already existing authoritarian system.

Thereafter, the repression of one's own opinions and feelings, along with automatic submission to superior authority, was made second nature to the Japanese by the systematic application of intense physical and psychological pressures, backed up by swift punishment for anyone who resisted.

The authoritarian nature of this feudal family system of enterprise management was greatly tempered, however, by the broad application of a philosophy of humanism which had also been a traditional characteristic of the Japanese since ancient times. This humanism was a fundamental belief, Shintō in origin, that people should be selfless and kind and help each other, that superiors are morally obligated to take care of those who work for or serve them, and that peaceful harmony should be maintained by strict adherence to these beliefs.

The Parent-Child Ethic
Japan's distinctive humanism-plus-authoritarianism business system was translated into action in the form of a parent-child relationship. The employer was looked upon as a combination mother and father, and the employees were the "children." Interpersonal relations between the two ideally followed the rearranged Confucian principles, just as they were applied to private family life in Feudal Japan.

For centuries people were taught to respect authority and to work cooperatively. In return for this, they were guaranteed a livelihood and protection. The system was held together and made to function by minutely defined personal obligations and a highly refined etiquette system. The focal points of the various controlling obligations were the central government (the Shogunate), the clan, the family, and finally the individual.

The introduction of limited individualism and democracy into Japan in 1867 weakened and in some cases completely severed these feudalistic, obligatory ties. With the changeover to an industrial economy in the 1870s and 1880s, the means of earning a living became the focal point in the lives of the Japanese. Company affiliation automatically replaced the clan, and to some extent the family as well, in the social fabric of the country. Business leaders inherited the loyalty, the respect, and the service once given to the clan and the feudal government.

The development of modern industry in Japan thus was a primary factor in the breaking up of the feudal patterns in home life. At the same time, the larger enterprises, especially, continued the functions of the old family and clan units. Each company comprised a great family of its own in which the traditional patterns of obligation, loyalty, and conduct continued in only slightly diminished force.

Still today Western business executives who approach large Japanese companies should keep in mind that they are dealing with a "family" in which the members are ranked vertically according to their seniority and position and that, with only rare exceptions, one member cannot commit the "family" to anything. Most Japanese executives on whatever level must obtain the advice and consent of their "company relatives."

The distinctive Japanese family-company system is changing rapidly under pressure from uncontrollable economic factors. Enough of it still remains, however, to give Japanese companies and Japanese company management a special character of their own.

Marine Corps Management
One of the best ways to gain a quick surface insight into traditional Japanese management philosophy and practices is to relate each company or organization to a military unit, particularly to the U.S. Marine Corps, in which rank and seniority are the foundation of all relationships.

Under this system, every "enlistment" in a major Japanese corporation is, in principle, for the working life of the individual. Those with grade school and high school education start as privates and eventually may become noncommissioned officers (blue-collar workers, supervisors, and foremen). University graduates automatically become officer candidates (management trainees) when they "enlist," and all expect to be promoted to successively higher officer ranks as they build up longevity.

With growing exceptions, pay scales are primarily based on longevity in service and rank, with promotions determined by time-in-grade, schooling, and other qualifications. The company lapel button is the "uniform" and the title on the name card denotes rank. The *ojigi,* or "bow," is the equivalent of the military salute. Inferiors have traditionally been expected to pay proper respect to superiors and to obey them without question—a handicap that a growing number of companies have recognized and now have programs designed to encourage employees to speak up individually.

Superiors are responsible for both the good and bad actions of their subordinates and can win and keep their respect and support only by taking care of them.

Just as the outsider generally does not enter the Marine Corps as a sergeant or captain, the Japanese company requires, with still only a few exceptions, that its noncommissioned members (blue collar workers) and officers (managers) come up through the ranks. They thus have a proper understanding and appreciation of the manners and ethics required by the company.

Just as different branches of the armed forces tend to compete with each other for everything from funds to research projects, so do Japanese companies. Within Japanese companies there is also the same sectional and departmental rivalry that was traditionally promoted in every military organization, from squads of foot soldiers up to armies.

Activities within sections and departments in Japanese companies are very much like those in a squad, platoon, or company of Marines, with similar attitudes toward responsibility and loyalty to their branch of service.

Just as military personnel are generally promoted to higher ranks according to their educational background (high school, university, and academy), they also concern themselves with dates of promotion. Within the rank of captain, for example, Captain Smith outranks Captain Jones because Smith was promoted first and therefore has more time-in-grade.

Just as a well-trained and highly motivated squad of marines can naturally be expected to do well in battle, a Japanese group does particularly well in situations demanding close, co-operative teamwork. As in the military, independent spirits or the innovators generally fare well in Japan only if they are capable of working within the group, forgoing personal ambitions and recognition. Attempts by individuals who are especially capable and ambitious to go out on their own are still rare enough that when they succeed on an impressive scale it makes national news.

Again, a primary advantage of the Japanese system of vertically ranking each individual and each group and the various rules that govern the system is that it can be galvanized for quick action and can be expected to perform like a well drilled infantry squad. All team members are responsible for their own as well as the livelihood of their teammates and regardless of how they personally feel about the people they work with or what they are charged with doing, they are under extraordinary pressure to do their best.

The Emotional-Sensual Element
Despite the cultural factors that make Japanese and Western executives different in attitudes, manners, and methods, most Westerners who spend considerable time in Japan become strongly attracted to living and working there.

This attraction is may be separated into two categories, the intellectual/emotional and the sexual. There are two sides and several facets to the intellectual/emotional category that appeals both consciously and subconsciously to Westerners. First is their appreciation of the manners and aesthetic elements in Japanese culture and second is their admiration for the Japanese work and management attributes that have made Japan so successful despite the fact that they view some of them critically.

There is also a very strong sense of the exotic and the sensual surrounding everything that has survived from Old Japan, and this added dash of the romantic and mysterious contributes to the aesthetic pleasure experienced by foreigners confronted with a traditional Japanese scene.

The sexual category pertains almost entirely to men, and applies especially to those who were steeped in the Puritan Christian concept that sex is basically sinful and that monogamy and/or abstinence are moral virtues. In Japan, sex has never had the stigma of sin. On the contrary, it has always been considered an important part of living; playing a vital role in the native religion of the country, as well as having been sanctioned as a pleasure. The guidelines were based on who, when and where.

There were traditionally different sexual moralities for men and women in Japan, however. Generally, all men considered that they had a right to unconcealed sexual promiscuity, the volume and variety depending only on what each individual could afford and wanted. Women, on the other hand, were divided into two groups: those known as "public women" who worked away from their homes in inns, tea houses, restaurants, drinking establishments, and redlight districts; and women who did not work outside their homes–the famous *O'josan* (Oh-joe-sahn)—who were brought up under very strict conditions and were usually, of course, the daughters of the well-to-do.

The *O'josan* and the wives of the privileged samurai warrior class, and in particular the nobility, were not ascetics, however. Throughout most of Japan's history, they engaged in love affairs whenever possible, and they were not subject to pangs of moral guilt or criticism stemming from a belief that virginity or marital faithfulness was a divine virtue. About the only difference between the public and "private" women of Japan, as far as their attitude toward sexual morality was concerned, was time, place, and partner.

In Old Japan, lower-class women, who were the majority, as well as women of rank, were pretty much at the mercy of the proud, haughty samurai who carried their male prerogative as far as their audacity and means would allow. The great chain of over 75,000 inns that flourished during the long Tokugawa era (1603-1868) functioned as nightly "lovetels." Legal and illegal red-light districts also flourished in Japan until April Fool's Day in 1956, with a one-year grace period to go out of business. [I and two friends marked this auspicious event by going to the Yoshiwara in Tokyo's Asakusa Ward, the most famous red-light district in the country.]

Today in Japan the situation is pretty much the same as far as volume and variety of sexual activities are concerned. There are no concentrated, marked pleasure quarters, but there are more "public girls," and the pampered daughters of the well-to-do are more apt to be abroad at night than the less fortunate young woman who works in some office or store. There is widespread sexual activity among students in their upper teens and above. A large number of news media covering the sensual side of life in Japan frequently documents the practice for female students to have older patron-lovers who pay them a regular retainer.

In addition to liaisons between customers of hostesses employed in bars and cabarets, there is also widespread sexual activity among couples in the business and social world who become acquainted and then date. This includes older married men, who are usually in a much better position to carry on an outside affair because of their higher income brackets.

Most of the *non-mizu shobai* women concerned are single, but it is not unusual for married women to have occasional or full-time lovers—especially since a significant percentage of their husbands not only carry on extramarital affairs but also often spend long periods away from home on company business.

There are thousands of inns and hotels throughout Japan that exist by renting rooms to couples who use them for only an hour or so. Most of the famous resort areas, such as Atami and Ito, depend to a considerable extent upon the weekend patronage of trysting couples to keep them flourishing. These very common weekend trips are often referred to as "weekend honeymoons," and many men who go on them regularly, with different women as often as possible. I have known a number of men who boasted they had had a different "weekend bride" almost every weekend for a period of several years.

Not having a sense of guilt about indulging in sex, the Japanese look at it in an entirely different light than what has been traditional among Christianized Westerners. At the same time, the idea that a woman who is not a virgin has endangered her chances of making a good marriage has been present in Japan since ancient times. It seems, however, that this belief is not nearly strong enough to counterbalance the other attitudes toward sex—one of which, in several parts of feudal Japan included "trial marriages" by couples who were attracted to each other. The boy and girl lived together, usually in the girl's home for a few weeks or months to find out if they could get along. If they couldn't, and the girl wasn't pregnant, the boy returned home and started looking elsewhere.

It should not be surprising, therefore, that when the average Western man finds himself in a society that still condones in practice, if no longer in principle, sexual promiscuity he is apt to take to it like a duck to water.

In addition to the attraction provided by actual sexual contact, there is a sensuality and sexuality pervading Japanese culture that gives off a constant promise of sex. This promise is a powerful stimulant to the average Western man, and it is the appeal of this distinctive atmosphere that holds many outsiders to Japan, rather than actual pleasures of the flesh.

One thing rambunctious foreign men who are newcomers to Japan should keep in mind is that Japanese girls and young women are no longer either pushovers or permissive in their attitude toward boyfriends and husbands. Divorces have become common—and in more notorious cases occur immediately after the honeymooning couple return to Japan through Narita Airport; resulting in the news media labeling them *Narita Rikon* [Nah-ree-tah Ree-kone] or "Narita Divorces."

The Kindness Syndrome
For every example of a bad or obnoxious habit or manner that the Japanese have (from the Western viewpoint) there is a good or pleasing characteristic can also be pointed to, and it is obvious that the good side outweighs the bad. In many years of living and working in Japan, I have had so many special kindnesses extended to me that at times it has been embarrassing. Foreign visitors to Japan invariably have a number of such experiences with the Japanese that are genuine—and sometimes startling—demonstrations of unselfish kindness.

Such incidents are common, and although the longtime foreign resident in Japan often takes them for granted, the newcomer is immensely impressed and enthusiastic in his praise for the Japanese. This very strong human element, which is characteristic of the Japanese when they are in their own environment and at peace with themselves and others, also helps make living and working in Japan pleasurable and often more satisfying than living back home.

Sources of Japan's Strength

In addition to the human element that cancels out many of the attitudes and habits of the Japanese that are negative and disadvantageous, there are other psychological and sociological factors that explain why the Japanese despite their failings are a formidable race and why Japan is one of the world's top industrial powers. The first and most important of these factors has been the willingness of the Japanese to sacrifice. From earliest times, the Japanese were taught and conditioned to believe that it was a virtue to devote their labor and their lives to fulfill the various obligations that were the essence of their society.

This willingness to sacrifice has been the one prevailing ethic by which the people lived through the centuries and which made possible the development of all the various attitudes and habits that distinguish the Japanese from other people. Until the coming of economic affluence in the 1960s, it was visible in every aspect of their society.

Along with this willingness to sacrifice came a willingness to be regimented and homogenized. The Japanese became alike mentally and socially to such an extent that they more or less functioned as a single unit, as one giant family with a common head. Another of the secrets of the nation's rise to the heady heights of world power is simply that almost everybody worked together for the same end for considerably less personal benefit than workers in other industrialized countries.

As already mentioned, another factor that also tempers to a great extent the harsher aspects of Japanese society and at the same time contributes to the industrial prowess of Japan is the very deep and broad stream of aestheticism permeating the traditional culture.

Factors that played leading roles in the development of an aesthetic civilization in Japan include the powerful influence of Shintō and Zen Buddhism. One of the most interesting of the Zen Buddhism influences was manifested in the tea ceremony, which is still widely practiced in Japan.

To those with only a cursory knowledge of Japan and the Japanese, describing the familiar sounding but little understood tea ceremony as anything more than "tea with some rules" may sound farfetched. However, to declare that the tea ceremony is one of the principal manifestations for much that is called "'Japanese" may sound strange, indeed. Nevertheless, it is so.

As practiced by the Japanese, the tea ceremony is essentially a worship of the natural and an attempt to achieve perfect harmony with nature and the cosmos. The tea room, the most important accessory in the tea ceremony, is a different world. It is free from all vulgarity, free from the slightest distraction, so that one can surrender completely to the adoration of natural beauty; to striving for physical and spiritual union with the cosmos.

As a result of the remarkable aesthetic sense of the Japanese, there is a subtle charm and in many cases an exquisite beauty in the basic form and decorative design of native Japanese products. It was the distinctive charm and beauty— called *shibui* [she-buu-ee] in Japanese—that captured the imagination of the Western world when Japan first became known to the West.

The aesthetic theme is still conspicuous in Japan today, although there is a tremendous gap between the attitudes and practices of older people and the younger generation. The theme is obviously weakening under the onslaught of Western products and ideas, but it is still there in the language, architecture, arts, crafts, and the remnants of the traditional life-style. It still provides the Japanese of all ages with a unique source of strength and satisfaction that is sorely lacking in other industrial societies.

Pride, Prejudice, and Perseverance

The Japanese have always been a proud people, and when they have the opportunity, they are just as ambitious. This pride and burning ambition to prove their superiority—or at least their equality—accounts for a great deal of their strength, energy and perseverance. They measure their accomplishments against the world's best or the largest. The more successful they are the more convinced they become that their way is the right way.

The Japanese have, in fact, long been virtually obsessed with their national character, and they still spend a great deal of time and money studying it. These studies show that the Japanese generally consider themselves happy and contented and that they regard themselves as the hardest working, most diligent, politest, kindest, and most patient people in the world. Typical Japanese executives are always very much concerned about upholding the honor of Japan and the Japanese in dealings with outsiders. In their own minds, they never act alone. They are acting for and are under the scrutiny of all Japanese.

It is still typical of Japanese executives to assume a humble stance in the presence visitors. This often gives resident or visiting Western executives a high feeling of superiority, and frequently leads them to underestimate the Japanese, and to commit excesses. The Japanese executive is simply being polite and treating the foreigner as an honored guest.

Virtually all management personnel in larger Japanese companies are university graduates and regard themselves as an elite group and as intellectuals. It is also characteristic of those who have gone into the government ministries to harbor a certain amount of cultural, racial, and political prejudice against the world at large and to regard themselves as Japan's first bulwark of defense against excessive foreign encroachment. They are not adverse, however, to learning all they can from outsiders and adapting the knowledge to their own advantage. In fact, the urge and need to do so is compulsive.

Japanese executives are deeply committed to the management system in their own company because, in the ways that count, their company is their life. The penalty for not conforming, for breaking the traditional pattern, is serious. If they should step out of line, they are either shunted aside or ostracized and unless they have powerful connections they have practically no chance of being taken in by another company of comparable standing.

Individually, Japanese executives are not bound by immutable principles of good, bad or logic in the Western sense. They adapt easily and readily to suit the circumstances and have a starkly realistic attitude toward power and what suits their (and Japan's) best interest. The old characteristics of abhorring selfishness and regarding profit making as a social evil have long since been relegated to the background.

Japanese businesspeople are usually more complex individuals than their Western counterparts and, in a different way, are subjected to a great deal more stress. Once they enter a large company as young people, they have very little direct control over their future. They must adhere to demanding etiquette and ethical codes in order to avoid upsetting the harmony of the system, knowing all the while that they will most likely spend their entire working life intimately linked to the same co-workers.

Traditionally, the Japanese management system was geared to obtain maximum cooperation from employees with a minimum of friction, with obtaining business results seemingly secondary. The fact that the system has survived and still works to a significant degree is obvious.

However, the Japanese are changing and becoming less "Japanese"—too slowly in the eyes of a growing number. In their view, among the several challenges now facing the Japanese is whether or not they can, in fact, change their national character fast enough and far enough to succeed in their goals of keeping Japan in the top tier of nations.

BUSINESS-RELATED WEBSITES

There are dozens of online sites offering a variety of information, services and resources on setting up and doing business in Japan.

Venturejapan.com
This private commercial site provides company incorporation, branch-office registration, executive recruitment, business management services, market-entry, PR, and marketing.

Eurotechnology.com/doing-business-in-Japan/
This site emphasizes the things that many foreign companies do wrong in approaching the Japanese market, beginning with

inadequate preparation and no strategy...and this includes large corporations that are successful elsewhere.

Doingbusiness.org/data/explore-economies/Japan/
Sponsored by the World Bank, this site provides basic information about the legal aspects of establishing and managing a company in Japan. For example, the procedures for establishing a company:

1) Make a company seal.

2) Acquire certificate of seal registration of representative managing member at the Ward office.

3) Register at the head office or a branch of the Legal Affairs Bureau of the Ministry of Justice.

4) File notification of the incorporation of a company, the opening of a payroll office, and application for the approval of blue tax returns with District Tax Office.

5) File notification of the commencement of business with the local tax office (the office of local or prefectural government).

6) File notifications of commencement the applied business and labor insurance, and the rules of employment with the Labor Standards Inspection Office.

7) File applications for health insurance and public welfare pension with the Social Insurance Office.

8) File application for business establishment of employment insurance with the Public Employment Security Office

Attorneys / Law Firms
http://www.hg.org/firms-japan.html

Chambers of Commerce in Japan
http://www.cin.or.jp/link/ccis/ccihmpg-e.html

Driver's Licenses / Driving Regulations
http://www.japan-guide.com/e/e2022.html

Export Laws
http://www.customs.go.jp/english/summary/export.htm

Foreign Embassies
http://www.mofa.go.jp/about/emb_cons/protocol/

Foreign Schools
http://japan.english-schools.org/

Hot Spring Spas
http://www.japan-guide.com/e/e2292_where.html

Immigration Laws
http://www.immi-moj.go.jp/english/

Import Laws
http://www.customs.go.jp/english/summary/import.htm

Incorporation Laws
http://www.juridique.jp/incorporation.html

Japanese Style Inns
http://www.japan-guide.com/e/e2029.html

Labor Laws
http://www.ilo.org/public/english/dialogue/ifpdial/info/national/jp.htm

Marriage Laws
http://japan.usembassy.gov/e/acs/tacs-7114a.html

National Holidays
http://www.officeholidays.com/countries/japan/default.asp

Real Estate Agents
http://www.jafnet.co.jp/index_en.html

Requirements for Permanent Residence
http://www.immi-moj.go.jp/english/tetuduki/zairyuu/eizyuu.html

Tax Laws
http://www.venturejapan.com/japanese-corporate-tax.htm

Visa Categories
http://www.jnto.go.jp/eng/arrange/essential/visa.html
http://www.us.emb-japan.go.jp/english/html/travel_and_visa/travel_and_visa_index.htm

PART 4

Other Key Terms In Japan's Business Vocabulary

Ago (ah-go) / In Japan, one leads by the *ago* (chin) instead of the nose, and instead of "turning up your nose," you "turn up your chin." The *ago* is used in various business contexts, such as when a superior disregards the feelings of subordinates and' 'drives them by the chin." By the same token, when an employee does his best but fails in a task, he has *ago wo dashimashita* (stuck his chin out to be hit).

Aisatsu (aye-sot-sue) / Usually translated into English as "greeting," *aisatsu* has a great deal more significance in its Japanese context than "greeting" implies. The Japanese attach considerable importance to meeting their business and professional contacts in a formal, ritualized manner, on a regular basis. Some *aisatsu* meetings are routine but important, and are used to introduce a new company member or new product or to express thanks for something special. The more important the occasion is, the higher ranking are the participants is the *aisatsu*. Prior to a major tie-up between companies, it is customary for the two presidents to hold a relatively short get-acquainted *aisatsu*. Specific details of the association are not discussed. The prime function of the high-level *aisatsu* is to put the official seal of approval on the proposed new relationship so that subordinate executives can thereafter work out the relationship in confidence. In some cases, the presidential *aisatsu* are not held until after the agreement has been worked out.

Aisatsu-mawari (aye-sot-sue-mah-wah-ree) / This literally means "to go around and greet or pay respects" to customers, clients, business contacts, and fellow workers, and it is an institutionalized custom after week-long New Year's holidays, as well as after the return of an individual to the home office from an overseas assignment. Such courtesy calls are an integral part of Japan's business etiquette and should be adopted by foreign businesspeople involved with the Japanese. It is also essential for foreign businesspeople to keep in mind that very little if any business is accomplished in or with Japanese companies during this period (usually a two or three-day period), beginning on January 4 or 5.

Aiso (aye-so) / The Japanese are noted for smiling a lot and for being exceptionally courteous and kind. Some of this behavior is, of course, sincere. Some of it, however, is professional and is called *aiso,* which is represented by the clerk, tradesmen or businesspeople who put on a smiling face when greeting and dealing with customers or potential clients. Foreign businesspeople should keep in mind that *aiso* is an art that the Japanese practice with considerable skill. They will often continue smiling when disappointed, shocked, or angry, which can be very misleading to someone not familiar with the Japanese way.

Aka chochin (ah-kah choe-cheen) / Literally, "red lantern," an *aka chochin* is a large globe-shaped lantern made of heavy paper pasted over a bamboo frame that is hung in the front of bars and other drinking places. It has become synonymous with nighttime entertainment. The red lights add an exotic touch to the nighttime scene in Japan's thousands of entertainment and bar districts. (See also, *Chotto ippai* and *Hashigo-zake.*)

Antei (ahn-tay-ee) / *Antei* is the sense of security/care Japanese workers expect to get from their employers. It includes explicit interest in their personal welfare outside the company and involvement in such matters as marriage and death.

Aota-gai (ah-oh-tah-guy) / Major Japanese companies generally hire new entry-level employees only once a year, directly from high schools and universities. High school graduates are employed as blue collar workers. University graduates are automatically slated for office jobs. In the days when there was a labor shortage, it became common for larger companies to begin recruiting college students a year or more before they were scheduled to graduate. This practice came to be known as *aota gai,* or "harvesting green plants."

Small and medium-sized enterprises in Japan complained bitterly about this practice and sought government help in establishing some order in the hiring process. Through government mediation, leading corporations in the country agreed to not invite job-seeking college seniors to visit them before October 1 and to not hold employment examinations before November 1.

From 50 to 60 violations of the agreement are reported to the Labor Ministry each year, but it is estimated that this reflects only a small percentage of the actual number of *aota-gai* cases annually. As observers note, as long as college seniors want to work for prestigious firms and those firms prefer to have first pick of each senior class, "green harvesting" will continue.

Asameshi-mae (ah-sah-may-she-my) / Literally "before breakfast, "this term is used to indicate that something that is to be done is so simple it can be done "before breakfast" -i.e., "as easy as pie." The term is used by people boasting of their ability, as well as by people who want to flatter someone into doing something extra (by telling them it will be *asameshi-mae* for them).

Ate-uma (ah-tay-uu-mah) / In its original usage, *ate-uma* referred to a stallion brought near a mare to excite her and make her ready for the studhorse that actually was to mate with her. Later it came to used in reference to any device, tool, draft plan, or technique to find out the true intentions of another company or party (with whom you want or plan to do business). If you are trying to sell a product or project to a certain company and mention that some other company is also interested in the deal, you are using the other company as an *ate-uma*.

Bansei-sho (bahn-say-show) / A "document of reflection," the *bansei-sho* is an official apology that the Japanese (or foreigners in Japan) are expected to write when they run afoul of the law. Individuals who express regret at having broken the law by writing a *bansei-sho* are generally given the benefit of the doubt and shown leniency-often being let off with a warning.

Banzai (bahn-zie) / Westerners are likely to associate this shout (which literally means "Ten thousand years!") with pre-World War II Japan and emperor worship (when it usually meant "Long live the Emperor!' '), but it is now more or less a shout of congratulations and goodwill, meaning "Bon voyage!" "Hip, Hip, Hurrah!" and so on. It is used when seeing newly wedded couples off on their honeymoon, executives off on overseas assignments, or when celebrating winning a sports event.

Base-up (bay-sue ah-puu) / This is an expression used mostly by unions in reference to their annual spring drives to win increases in the base wages of workers. (See also *Shunto*.)

Besso (base-soh) / This is a villa usually in the mountains or on the seacoast originally for recreational or retirement purposes of the well-to-do. Now, many *besso* are owned by companies and made available to employees as a fringe benefit.

Boryoku ba (boe-rio-kuu bah) / This literally means a "violence bar" and refers to bars controlled by the underworld that charge unwary customers outrageous prices for their drinks (often several hundred dollars for a few drinks) and use force, if necessary, to collect from their victims. Out-of-town Japanese often become victims of this system because they almost never ask the price of anything before they buy it (because of a combination of misplaced pride and reluctance to appear "cheap"). Foreign visitors to Japan also sometimes wander into these places and order without inquiring about the price. If the price is not posted on a wall or on a menu, ask. If it is too much, walk out.

Bottoru-kipu (bote-toe-rue-keep-puu) / In the late 1950s it became common for Japanese businessmen to buy bottles of Scotch (usually) at favorite bars and have them kept there ("bottle-keep"). When they patronized these bars, they paid only for set ups (which can be more expensive than a drink in typical bars outside Japan). The system was popular because it was another way of becoming a member of a group and having" face" in the entertainment world. Businesspeople frequently took foreign guests to their *bottoru-kipu* bars. The custom is now rare.

Bucho dairi (buu-choe die-ree) / *Dairi* means "agent," "deputy," or "assistant." A *bucho dairi* is therefore an assistant department head. A *kacho dairi* is a deputy section chief.

Bureiko (buu-ray-koe) / Social and business etiquette in Japan is such that, during the normal course of activity, there are strict rules of behavior that prevent people from being informal and casual. This deeply ingrained social system prevents people from being themselves and from developing close, personal relationships during working hours. To counter this, the system provides brief periods when the rules of etiquette may be ignored or broken. This is known as going *bureiko,* or without etiquette, and applies to such events as year-end and New Year's parties, athletic field meets, and nighttime drinking sessions. *Bureiko* is made up of three compounds or words that mean "absence," "respect," and "form." *Burei* is usually translated as "impoliteness" or "rudeness." *Bureiko* can also be translated as an "informal party."

Chochin kiji (choe-cheen kee-jee) / A *chochin* is a paper lantern and a *kiji* is a newspaper article. A *chochin kiji* is an article that "sheds light" on some company product or topic and refers to news articles that are favorable to a company or individual. Such articles often accompany advertisements, sometimes appearing on the same page or at least in the same section of the publication as the ad. A *chochin kiji* is the Japanese version of a "puff article."

Chorei Shiki (choe-ray she-kee) / The *Chorei Shiki,* "Morning Greeting Ceremony," was a traditional custom in the offices of most larger Japanese companies. The employees stood, faced the manager, bowed to one another, and called out morning greetings. The manager then ordinarily made announcements or comments on whatever is appropriate. In some companies, these morning sessions included rousing pep talks and ended with the singing of company songs. The ceremonies were an important part of the group orientation and communal spirit of Japanese management. Now some companies have dispensed with them altogether. In others they are less formal and shorter.

Chotto ippai (cho-toe eep-pie) / This is a colloquial phrase that has come to mean "Let's have a quick drink." It is another institutionalized practice that plays a key role in interpersonal relations of company employees. Since frank and personal conversations are almost never held in the office during working hours, the custom is to have one, two, or three drinks after hours and talk about concerns or problems in an informal atmosphere. A great deal of Japan's business communication takes place during *chotto ippai* sessions at bars.

Chotto muzukashi (cho-toe muu-zuu-kah-she) / When a Japanese businessperson, politician, or anyone else says, *"chotto muzukashi"* ("It's a little difficult"), it is usually a polite way of saying "no," "it can't be done," or "I can't do it." Not understanding the true meaning of the term, foreign executives are likely to continue trying aggressively to get the Japanese executives to accept or agree to whatever they want, even though it is a little difficult. The foreigner's presentation often includes how it can be done "easily."

Chuto saiyo (chuu-toe sie-yoe) / Larger Japanese companies normally hire only once a year in the spring directly from schools (see also *Teiki-saiyo*). When they do hire at other times during the year and this is usually only in the case of a special need or emergency, such as a sudden expansion or the need for someone highly skilled in a special area, it is known as *chuto saiyo* or "midstream hiring." Employees hired during midstream by larger firms, especially if they have worked for other companies, may be regarded as something less than pure company people for the rest of their working careers.

Daikoku bashira (die- koe- kuu bah -she-rah) / The literal meaning of *daikoku bashira* is something like "good fortune divinity pillar," which came to mean the main pillar in a building or house that holds up the entire structure. It is now often used in reference to an especially capable or productive individual or product on which a company or organization depends. Despite the diffusion of responsibility and achievement in the typical Japanese group, there is often a single, outstanding individual who is recognized as the group's *daikoku bashira* and to whom the group will defer. A product that is responsible for a significant percentage of company sales is also referred to as a *daikoku bashira*.

Dame-oshi (dah-may-oh-she) / *Dame* by itself means something is "no good" or "bad" or "useless." With the addition of *oshi,* the term means "to make sure" or "to confirm." It is a very important word in doing business in Japan because it is expected and customary for people to reconfirm delivery, shipping dates, appointments, and decisions. The implication is that circumstances may change unexpectedly.

Danketsu (dahb-kate-sue) / Literally "union" or "combination," this term is used in reference to the unity that the Japanese see as one of the primary sources of the energy they apply to business.

Danshijugyo-in (dahn-she-juu-ghee-yoe-een) / All the male employees below the rank of *kacho* (section chief).

Datsu-sara (dot-sue-sah-rah) / This literally means "to get away from a salary," and it refers to the recent trend for more and more younger and middle-aged Japanese salaried personnel to quit the corporations they work for and go out on their own—still an unconventional and controversial thing to do.

Dorai (doe-rye) / This is the English word "dry." The Japanese adopted it to mean the kind of impersonal, profit-oriented approach to business attributed to Western businesspeople. Conversely, their *ninjo* (human feelings) oriented business system is regarded as "wet" (wet-toe). The same words are also applied to one's attitude toward members of the opposite sex...with females being mostly wet and males being mostly dry.

Doru-bako (doe-rue-bah-koe) / This is literally "dollar-box," a take-off on *kane-bako* (money-box). It is a slightly dated term is used in reference to a company's most profitable product, business line, or department. It is also used in reference to a financial backer who becomes someone's *doru-bako*.

Dosa mawari (doe-sah mah-wah-ree) / Originally "touring around" and applied to theatrical troupes, *dosa mawari* now refers to an individual in a company who is rotated to two or more provincial offices or branches in succession (and is usually used in a negative sense). Since employees are fired in Japan only under extreme circumstances, head offices often assign undesirable individuals to branches or subsidiaries on a permanent basis, a process known as *tobasareta* (toe-bah-sah-ray-tah) (being kicked out), instead of firing them.

Dosatsu ryoku (doe-sot-sue ree-yoe-kuu) / Able to "see through things," to have "keen insight." It is a quality the Japanese look for in a top executive.

Dososei (doe-soh-say-ee) / Japanese businesspeople probably network more than any others in the world, but they do it only within very specifically defined groups with which they have well established bonds. Often the most important of these groups is their *dososei* or alumni brothers. A lot of business in Japan occurs only because individuals have alumni in other companies. When Japanese workers begin to think about developing a relationship with another company, they are most likely to consider first whether or not they have an alumnus in the other firm. Foreign businesspeople in Japan who are graduates of Japanese universities have a decided advantage in being able to count large numbers of Japanese businesspeople as their "soul mates."

Fuku shacho (fuu-kuu shah-choe) / A *fuku shacho* is a vice president, a title that is not very common in Japan. In Japanese companies, the role of the vice-president in the Western sense is more likely filled by a director.

Fundoshi hitotsu de (foon-doe-she he-tote-sue day) / Literally, "with one *fundoshi*. " A *fundoshi* is a narrow loincloth and is the traditional Japanese equivalent of "shorts" or "panties" as the case may be. The *phrase fundoshi hitotsu de* is an old one and refers to starting a company or project with little or no capital-on a G-string instead of a shoestring.

Futokoro-gatana (fuu-toe-koe-roe-gah-tah-nah) / Literally a "breast-dagger" (which in feudal Japan was the knife used by samurai to commit *hara-kiri* or ritual suicide). The word may now be used to refer to the "right-hand man" of a boss or one who is totally trusted and functions as an executive's chief of staff. The term is a complimentary one.

Gaijin (guy-jeen) / An "outside person," this is the Japanese word for "foreigner." You hear it often in Japan because the Japanese habitually distinguish between Japanese and non-Japanese. The connotation of the word has long been derogatory, so speakers often add the word *kata*, very polite for "person," to it: *gaijin-no kata* or "foreign person."

Gashi-kokan (Gah-she-koe-khan) / *Gashi-kokan* are Happy New Year parties staged by industrial associations and other business organizations for several days after offices reopen following New Year's. The purpose of the parties is to make it convenient for businesspeople to meet large numbers of their associates to wish everyone a Happy New Year and ask for their continued goodwill, cooperation, and business during the New Year. *Gashi-kokan* (which are also called *meishi-kokan* or "exchanging business cards") are normally held during the day. They invariably involve numerous toasts with *sake* or beer, leaving the participants red-faced and sweating.

Gekokujo (gay-koe-kuu-joe) / "To go over the head of one's superior." In feudal days this was something that could result in one literally losing his head. The practice is still very much frowned on in contemporary Japan and frequently acts as a barrier to business.

Go-en (go-inn) / The exclusive, group-oriented nature of Japanese society that makes it necessary for them to have *en* (relations) with an individual or company before they can do business with them. *En* is also the medium or cause that results in relations being established between groups. Two companies cannot engage in business without *en* having been established, and this necessary relationship cannot be established with a phone call. It requires introductions and a series of face-to-face meetings.

Goma-suri (go-mah-sue-ree) / As a society with a highly refined social etiquette and strict rules governing interpersonal relations, the Japanese have developed numerous techniques for smoothing human relations and making other people feel good. One of these techniques is known as *goma-suri,* which literally means" grinding sesame seeds, but is used figuratively to mean flattering someone. The Japanese often act embarrassed when paid compliments, but they themselves pay compliments at the drop of a single Japanese word or if you manage to put one bite of food into your mouth with chopsticks. Foreigners not used to the kind of effusive *goma-suri* practiced by the Japanese are often put off balance and made more vulnerable.

Goshugi torihiki (go-shuu-ghee toe-ree-he-kee) / *Shugi* means "celebration" or "congratulations" and *torihiki* means "business." Put together they refer to giving a company some business to help it celebrate a special occasion (like an opening or an anniversary or the first day of business after New Year's). This is a traditional and honored custom in Japan and is part of the Japanese way of incorporating a strongly personal element into their business practices.

Gote-ni mawaru (go-tay-nee ma-wah-rue) / Derived from the game of *go,* this figuratively means "to get behind" or "be behind." In a business context, it refers to letting your competitor or negotiating counterpart get one up on you.

Gyosei-shido (ghee-yoe-say-she-doe) / This is the famous (or infamous) "administrative guidance" of business, practiced by bureaucrats in several key government ministries. The guidance consists of forcing or persuading businesspeople to follow certain policies or guidelines that are not required by law but are believed by the bureaucrats to be in the interest of the country. The pressure the ministries can bring to bear on individual companies, as well as on industries, is enormous.

Hae-nuki (hie-nuu-kee) / The word for' 'true-born," *hae-nuki* refers to a person who entered a company right out of school and has never worked anywhere else. It confers a special status upon individuals in that category. It ranges from difficult to impossible for a person who has worked elsewhere to join a new, large company and be fully accepted by *hae-nuki* employees. .

Hakurai suhai (hah-kuu-rie sue-hie) / Literally "the worship of foreign goods," this term is used in reference to the attraction that high-quality, famous name-brand imported goods have for the Japanese. The concept and the fascination go back to the - 1870s, when Japan began trading with the West after more than 200 years of self-imposed isolation. Some Japanese still buy imported goods just because they are foreign, but most consumers consider quality and after-service first.

Hame wo hazusu (hah-may oh hah-zuu-suu) / Literally "pull out all of the stops." This term is in reference to "letting one's hair down" and engaging in unrestrained drinking and merry-making at company parties when out drinking with fellow workers at night. Anyone who does not or cannot *hame wo hazusu* is suspect in Japan. Such people are likely to be regarded as unfriendly, arrogant, and hiding their real selves.

Hanko (hahn - koe) / These are the "chops" or "seals" the Japanese may use in lieu of their signature when signing documents or papers. There are three kinds of *hanko:* the *Jitsu-in,* or registered seal, for legal or official documents; the *Mitome-in,* or private seal, for everyday transactions, such as signing receipts or accepting registered mail and the like; and the *Ginko-in,* or bank seal, for bank transactions. Registered seals usually include the owner's full name, while the private ones usually have only the family name.

Since *hanko,* especially *the Jitsu-in,* represent the official signature of the owner, special care must be taken to ensure that they do not fall into the hands of anyone who would misuse them. The *hanko* are pressed first on a vermilion ink pad and then on the document. (In feudal Japan, only the samurai and aristocrats were allowed to use red ink. Commoners had to use black ink.) Quite a few foreigners who are permanent residents of Japan have *hanko* made and registered.

Hara-gei (hah-rah-gay-ee) / *Hara-gei* is the art of doing business "from the stomach," because the Japanese traditionally believed that the stomach was the center of a person's being and emotions. The word *hara* also appears in a number of other words and phrases that are regularly used in business: *hara wo miseru,* to show the stomach or reveal what is on one's mind; *hara wo watte hanasu,* to cut open the stomach or have a heart-to-heart talk; *hara wo kukuru,* to bundle up the stomach or become resolved to a situation and make the best of it; *hara ga tatsu,* the stomach stands up-i.e., to get angry; one is *hara-guroi* (one has a "black stomach" -i.e., is wicked, crafty). One who does business on *hara-gei* depends upon "gut feeling"—which is sometimes characterized as being subtle, devious, and/or cunning. The word is not used daily, but the practice is common.

Hashigo-zake (hah-she-go-zah-kay) / Until the economic meltdown that began in the late 1980s it was a deeply entrenched custom for Japanese office workers, especially those who have started up the rungs of the corporate promotional ladder, to go out in groups after work to drink, relax, get to know one another, air grievances, and otherwise blow off steam that builds up during the day. These groups usually went to several drinking places, getting higher as they go along—a process popularly known as *hashigo-zake* or *hashigo-nomi*, literally "ladder drinking." Because the Japanese are conditioned not to reveal their true thoughts and character while sober and on the job, these institutionalized evening drinking bouts served as an important adjunct to communication and maintenance of good personal relations within companies.

As of the slow-down in Japan's economic growth in the 1990s, and a growing practice for younger office workers to take more responsibility for their families, many of them now choose to go home directly after work. Still, afterhours drinking remains an essential part of the lives of the Japanese, with one new element that really took off in the 1970s: the large number of women who also patronize the beer gardens, hotel lounges, and *izakaya* [ee-zah-kah-yah]—combination restaurant-taverns of which there are several hundred thousand in the country.

Hatarakibachi (hah-tah-rah-kee-bah-chee) / This is the Japanese word for workaholic. It is not heard as often as one might expect, perhaps because everyone is expected to work hard.

Hataraku (hah-tah-rah-kuu) / This is the Japanese word for work. It is made up of compounds that mean "give rest to other people." The root meaning of *hataraku* implies that the Japanese regard work as a service to others, as opposed to a task they perform for their own personal benefit.

Hijikake-isu (he-jee-kah-kay-ee-sue) / It is usually possible to spot the managers in a Japanese office by their chairs. As soon as people are promoted to *kakaricho,* the first rung on the managerial ladder, each moves up to an armchair. The higher they go up the executive ladder, the larger and more comfortable their chair. Directors and presidents usually have *hijikake-isu* (arm-rest chairs), leather-upholstered chairs that are for sitting in and thinking rather than working in.

Hi-no-kuruma (he-no-kuu-rue-mah) / When people or companies in Japan suffer from financial difficulties, they are said to be on a *hi-no-kuruma,* or "fire car" (or cart), which is the vehicle used in Buddhist hell to transport dead sinners.

Hiru-andon (he-rue on-doan) / In earlier times the typical Japanese corporation, presidents, general managers, and department heads often played only a minor role in day-to-day management, leaving that to their deputies or assistants. These symbolic heads were sometimes referred to as *hiru andon,* or "day lamps," the idea being that you cannot tell whether or not a light is turned on during daylight hours. Such people often appeared to have no duties or obligations, and it does not seem to make any difference whether or not they are there. The Japanese have traditionally preferred this system as part of management by consensus.

Hito hada nugu (he-toe hah-dah nuu-guu) / This literally means "to remove one layer of skin." Figuratively, it means to do someone a favor without expecting anything in return or to repay a past favor (reluctantly).

Hitori-zumo (he-toe-ree-zuu-moe) / Sumo wrestling is Japan's traditional national sport. *Hitori-zumo* is a "one-man sumo match." It refers to people who take on very difficult tasks by themselves, without getting anyone to help them, and who end up running around in circles, working very hard, but failing. Foreigners who are not familiar with the group approach in Japan often try to persuade individuals in Japanese companies to take on products or programs as their own personal projects without realizing they are asking the people to engage in *hitori-zumo.*

Hiya-meshi-kui (he-yah-may-she-kuu-ee) / In a business or government office context, a person who has been made into a *hiyameshi-kui,* or "cold-rice-eater," has been shuffled aside into a powerless, meaningless position. People who have been pushed back or off the promotional ladder often complain of being forced to eat *hiya-meshi.* Foreign businesspeople who approach] apanese companies without impressive introductions and advance preparations are sometimes shuffled off onto *hiya-meshi-kui.*

Ho-toku (hoe-toe-kuu) / Perhaps more than any other people, the Japanese are imbued with a sense of *toku,* or virtue, which traditionally has been a part of their religious and educational upbringing. In addition to contributing to their sense of Japaneseness and nationhood, this conditioning has also helped shape their sense of social and economic obligation and is responsible in part for their cooperative approach to life and for the low level of violence in the country. Instruction in virtue was an integral part of life in feudal Japan. After the feudal system officially ended in 1868, the teaching of virtue was incorporated into the educational curriculum, and *Ho-toku,* or "the way of virtue," societies were formed. The way of virtue is still important in the making of the Japanese.

Insei (inn-say-ee) / In old Japan, *insei* referred to the system under which an emperor retired but continued to rule from behind the scenes. Nowadays it refers to businesspeople or politicians who have retired but continue to exercise authority and power in their former company or organization. The situation is very common, especially in politics and in companies where the retiree is the founder. A similar term is *O-gosho,* which originally meant the residence of a retired *shogun* (military dictator). Today it refers to the most prominent and powerful individual ("the top person") in any area of endeavor, including business, politics, or the arts.

Ippai yarimasho (eep-pie yah-ree-mah-show) / This literally means "let's have a drink," with it understood that the person making the suggestion wants to talk to the other person privately and/or frankly, or wants to develop a closer relationship with the individual or show appreciation. In other words, the person making such an invitation usually always has some purpose beyond just relaxing and drinking. (See *Chotto ippai.*)

Iro-ke (ee-roe-kay) / By itself *iro* means "color" and by extension, "sex," "love," "desire" or "interest." *Ke* means more or less "slight tinge." When attached to *iro,* the combination means a tinge of sexual awareness or interest. A businessperson who shows some interest in an idea or project may be described as *iro-ke wo misete-iru,* or showing signs of interest. Anyone who wants something badly is often described as *iro-ke tappuri,* or "full of desire."

Iro wo tsukeru (ee-roe oh t'sue-kay-rue) / This basically means "to apply color" and is used to mean "give special consideration to" to "fix up," "take care of," or "do something for somebody." It is often used in business in reference to negotiations or wage bargaining, when one side volunteers to add a little extra to the arrangement. In colloquial usage, *iro* means sexually attractive. An *iro-otoko* is a handsome (sexy) man. When used by itself, *iro* can mean lover or sweetheart.

Isekki mokeru (ee-say-kee moe-kay-rue) / To take someone to a bar, restaurant or geisha house in order to get on friendly terms prior to discussing business—the word is archaic, but the practice is very up to date.

Ishin denshin (ee-sheen dane-sheen) / This is usually translated as "tacit understanding" or "telepathy," and it is used in reference to nonverbal communication, a very important part of both social and business intercourse in Japan. As an ancient, sophisticated culture with a detailed and highly stylized etiquette, the Japanese are very sensitive to nonverbal communication, ranging from the well-known bow to the action of leaning back, closing their eyes, and appearing to be dozing or at least paying no attention during business negotiations. They *are* resting, but they are also thinking about what has been said and planning what to say next. The uninitiated Westerner is likely to become frustrated and possibly angered by such behavior. The literal meaning of *ishin denshin* is "what the mind thinks the heart transmits."

Jibara wo kiru (jee-bah-rah oh kee-rue) / This literally means "to cut one's own stomach," but it does not refer to the form of ritual suicide practiced in feudal Japan. Instead, it refers to a boss or manager paying for nighttime entertainment for his subordinates with his own money (as opposed to a company allowance). The purpose behind this ritual practice is to promote goodwill, cooperation, and loyalty among groups that work together in companies.

Jihyo (jee-h'yoe) / It is almost as difficult for a key figure to quit a major Japanese company as it is to be employed by one. A key individual who wants to resign or quit must submit a formal letter *called jihyo,* which the company may or may not accept. The company has no legal hold over an employee but can bring considerable pressure against anyone wanting to leave. A firm's efforts to prevent employees from leaving may have nothing to do with their abilities or real value. The effort may be, and often is, based on the desire to maintain the integrity and continuity of the lifetime employment system and to prevent the practice of leaving one firm for another from becoming common. If a company does not accept a *jihyo* and the people leave anyway, it becomes a serious black mark in their record that might later haunt them. If the resignation is accepted, however, it is accepted as an *en-man-taisha,* or "harmonious retirement."

Jingi wo kiru (jeen-ghee oh kee-rue) / Altogether, *jingi* means "humanity benevolence justice righteousness," regarded in Confucian terms as the basic principles of morality. In feudal Japan, *jingi* became the ethical code of the samurai and was eventually taken over by the *yakuza,* Japan's organized crime groups, which made it the basis for the relationship between gang leaders and their followers. The *yakuza* began using the *phrase jingi wo kiru* (to *cut jingi*) to describe the distinctive way they introduce themselves (with special gestures and facial expressions). Nowadays, companies planning to introduce a new product line in competition with other companies already in the field will go to these companies and *jingi wo kiri— that* is, introduce themselves and say they want to cooperate to avoid excessive competition. Companies will also make such introductory visits to other firms in the same line of business when they entice employees away from them. When used by businesspeople in these circumstances, the phrase has a negative feeling, since it describes an obligation that can be very unpleasant.

Jinji-ido (jeen-jee-e-doe) / Every year in March (just before the end of the fiscal year for most companies), Japanese corporations transfer dozens to hundreds of their employees from one department or division to another in an ongoing process to give them as much experience as possible. This particularly applies to those being groomed as top managers. Companies whose fiscal year ends in December usually conduct their *jinji-ido* (personnel transfers) in October. Managerial candidates who have reached the age at which a promotion is in order are especially anxious about the *jinji-ido* because their new post will tell them if they are still on track or if they are being shuffled aside to posts that are off the main line. The custom of *jinji-ido* is of specific interest to foreign executives dealing with Japanese companies because it means that every few years their key contacts are changed. This means they have to repeatedly go through the process of getting acquainted with new sub-managers and managers and developing good relations with them. It is especially important to keep this in mind during the spring months and in the fall, just before and just after the *jinji-ido* takes place. Foreign executives frequently find themselves in the position of having started a project with a group of people only to find they face an entirely new group, sometimes while the project is being negotiated.

Jin-myaku (jeen-me-yah-kuu) / This literally means the "pulse of a person," but it is used in the sense of personal connections, with the connotation being that good business (or personal) relations depend on having good personal contacts. Generally speaking, the Japanese will not engage in business with people from another company unless they have been introduced to them by one *of their jin-myaku* (personal connections). It is often said that the biggest asset that executives can have in Japan is a wide circle of *jin-myaku*. Foreign businesspeople who want to succeed in Japan must also develop their own circle of personal connections and must work constantly to keep them alive and well.

Jirei (jee-ray) / This is the official document that the personnel departments of larger companies and government bureaus issue to individuals to inform them that they have been hired, transferred, reassigned, retired, or fired. Once *a jirei* has been issued, there is generally no appeal, no matter how upsetting or unfair it might seem to an employee. *Jirei* are normally issued in the spring, when the companies and government bureaus take in batches of just graduated college students. In the case of ranking corporation executives or government officials, news of appointments and dismissals are sometimes leaked to newspapers, in which case they are known as *shimbun (newspaper) jirei,* and are not necessarily final. The spring season is understandably a period of tension and fear for many Japanese workers.

Joshi jugyo-in (joe-she juu-ghee-yoe-een) / The female employees of a company. It is still rare to find women in management positions in major Japanese companies. The most common exceptions are found in the service industries and in foreign companies in Japan.

Kaigi (kie-ghee) / A meeting, or conference, of which there are many kinds in Japan. In their meetings, particularly for the purpose of negotiating business arrangements, the Japanese seem to be most comfortable with groups of about ten persons, with all allowed to have their say. Such meetings most often start out in a relaxed, informal way. The custom of discussing every possibility and repeating the same questions in slightly different ways often results in talks going on for days or weeks and sometimes for months. Meetings play a decisive role in the consensus approach to decisions.

Kaki-ire-doki (kah-kee-ee-ray-doe-kee) / The literal meaning of this term is "time to write in" (sales entries or items put up for collateral), but it is now used to mean "the most profitable time" and refers to the major sales periods in department stores and other retailers (especially the two major gift-buying seasons" *O'chugen* [oh-chu-gain] in midsummer and *O'seibo* [oh-say-e-boe] in December), as well as the best sales periods of manufacturers and other businesses. When negotiating deals with Japanese companies, it is often helpful to know their *kaki-ire-doki*.

Kakushi-gei (kah-kuu-she-gay-ee) / Literally "hidden art," *kakushi-gei* refers to a special skill or talent that one has practiced in secret so as to be able to put on a good show when called upon to perform in public—which the Japanese are often required to do. The most common *kakushi-gei* are singing and folk dancing, but they might be acrobatics, mime, imitations, or some other skill that can be performed before an audience. Another old word for *kakushi-gei* is *ohako,* which *means juhachi-ban* or "number eighteen," and refers to the eighteen best plays of the legendary Ichikawa family of *kabuki* actors. The word is read as *hako,* meaning "box," apparently because the Ichikawa's kept the manuscripts of the eighteen plays in a safety box.

Kami (kah-me) / This is the word for "god" (usually written with a small *g),* which is synonymous with divine spirit and, in ordinary usage, with "the greatest" or "the best." Individuals who are regarded as the best in their field are often referred to as "the god of sales," "the god of baseball," "the god of movie-making."

Kanban (kahn-bahn) / In ordinary usage, *kanban* means "sign" or "bulletin board," but in business it has come to mean "just in time parts delivery," a management technique that was pioneered by Sakichi Toyoda. He was the founder of Toyoda Automatic Loom Works Ltd., the predecessor of Toyota Motor Corporation, in the 1920s and continued by his son and successor Kiichiro Toyoda in the 1930s. [The disparity in the spelling of the family name [Toyoda/Toyota] was a result of the clerk preparing the incorporation documents inadvertently choosing the character for ta instead of da.] The process was perfected in the years following the end of World War II (1945) by Taiichi Ono, manager (and later vice-president) of Toyota Motor Company Ltd., which had replaced Toyoda Automatic Loom Works Ltd. In 1978, Ono wrote a book describing the "just in time" system: *Toyota Seisan Hoshiki (The Toyota System of Production),* which was published by Diamond.

The use of the word *kanban* grew out of the fact that every morning Toyoda would put a list of all the parts and supplies that would be needed for the day on a big bulletin board on the floor of his loom factory.

Kangaete okimasu (kahn-guy-eh-tay oh-kee-mahss) / This literally means "I will think about it," but when a Japanese businessman, or anyone else, says it to you following some kind of approach or presentation, it invariably means no.

Kangei kai (kahn-gay kie) / *Kangei kai,* or "welcome parties," are an important part of employee relations in Japanese companies. *Kangei kai* are held when new employees enter a company, when individuals are assigned to new departments, when staff members return from overseas assignments, and various other occasions. Such parties are marked by drinking, eating, and merrymaking, and are aimed at developing and strengthening group identity and loyalty. (See also *Sobetsu kai.)*

Kanri shoku (kahn-ree show-kuu) / There is much less distinction between the *kanri shoku,* or "managerial level," and ordinary workers in Japanese companies. Lower and middle level managers generally do not have private offices or secretaries; all employees usually dress alike, and in general are indistinguishable from staff members except for age and seating arrangement. Managers sit at the head of rows of desks. The oldest person in the office is usually the ranking individual.

Kanryo shugi (kahn-rio shuu-ghee) / A term referring to the attitudes and manners associated with bureaucrats, i.e., "bureaucratic."

Kao (kah-oh) / Kao means "face." Besides the deeply felt need of the Japanese to *kao tateru* (save face), "face" is very important in other business contexts. A person who is well known and has many business contacts is one whose *kao ga hiroi* (face is wide). The person who has many contacts must work to keep them fresh and strong and spends a lot of time *Kao wo tsunagu* (tying up or fastening his face). If someone says *kao wo kashite* (lend me your face), it means he wants to talk to you and get your help.

Karaoke (kah-rah-oh-kay) / Literally "empty orchestra," *Karaoke* [kah-rah-oh-kay] is a type of singing into a microphone hooked up to speakers in concert with recorded orchestra music. The singer thus sings along with the "orchestra." *Karaoke* singing became popular in Japan in the early 1970s, and quickly spread to the bars and lounges where company employees gathered by the hundreds of thousands each night after work.

Throughout the 1970s and 80s a significant percentage of Japanese regularly patronized *karaoke* bars and took pride in their ability to belt out several songs, often in English as well as Japanese. The practice has diminished dramatically but is still popular among large numbers of people. Foreign visitors to Japan who want to develop deep rapport with their Japanese colleagues will come prepared to take their turn if and when invited to such bars.

Kasei (kah-say-ee) / *Kasei* refers to an office section or small department, the organizational basis for virtually all Japanese companies. Several *ka* combine to make a *bu* [buu] a larger department or division. The manager of a section is a *kacho* [kah-choe]. The assistant manager is a *kakaricho* [kah-kah-ree-choe]. The manager of a department or division is a *bucho* [buu-choe]. There may be only two or three people in a section of a small company and a dozen or more in larger companies. In many ways the *kacho* are among the most important people in a Japanese company. The research for most plans and projects is done by the *ka,* and most staff work is accomplished under the direction of the *kacho.* On the other hand, *bucho* spend most of their time chairing or attending intra-department or division meetings. In larger companies, *bucho* are the equivalent of vice-presidents in Western firms as far as rank and privilege are concerned, but they are generally not directly involved in creating programs, leaving that up to the section chiefs. One of differences between the activities and responsibilities of Japanese *bucho* and American or European vice-presidents is that the *bucho* seldom have secretaries, since they do very little that makes them necessary or useful.

Kayui tokoro ni te ga todoku (kah-yuu-ee toe-koe-roe nee tay gah toe-doe- kuu) / Japanese hotels, shops, and other places of business are rightfully famous for the variety and degree of service they provide to their customers. The degree and importance of this service are emphasized by the phrase *kayui tokoro ni te ga tqdoku,* which means "to scratch where it itches." The implication is that few things feel better than for someone to scratch you in an itchy place that you can't reach, and that it is up to people in business, especially those in the service industry, to know exactly where, when, and how to "scratch" customers to please them the most.

Keibatsu (kay-ee-bot-sue) / *Batsu* means "group," "faction," or "clique," and it is a very important word in the businessman's vocabulary, since most individuals and companies are members of and work within specific groups as teams. Virtually all activity in larger Japanese companies is on a group basis. *Kei* refers to "family" and, when used in combination with *batsu,* has the meaning of nepotism or family ties. Family ties and connections play a vital role in getting employment in the most desirable companies and government ministries and in rising in the social and political hierarchies. Most Japanese do not feel secure except as members of a group, and individually they are often unable to cope with conflicting situations. As part of this insecurity, most Japanese have difficulty accepting personal criticism. They are inclined to take such criticism as hostile and aimed at all Japanese, not just themselves.

Keiko (kay-ee-koe) / A term that used to mean "studying" or "considering old things, *keiko* is now used in reference to studying traditional artistic or martial arts skills, such as flower-arranging, playing the *koto,* or practicing judo or fencing. Learning how to sing is also regarded as *keiko.* Most large Japanese companies offer various *keiko* to their employees.

Keiretsu kaisha (kay-rate-sue kie-shah) / *Keiretsu* means "affiliated" or "series," and *kaisha* means "company." This term refers to the grouping of companies in Japan, including parent companies, subsidiaries, and subcontract firms, as well as those grouped around a certain bank or trading company. The system is an outgrowth of the economic structure of feudal Japan when older employees of businesses were allowed to go out and establish their own companies while maintaining close ties with their former employers. Members of specific company groups cooperate with one another in various ways, in what often amounts to an exclusive network. The group a particular company belongs to can be a vital factor in its dealings with foreign companies.

Kenami ga yoi (kay-nah-me gah yoe-ee) / Literally "good stock," as in a dog or horse with good bloodlines, but it is also frequently used in reference to a person who has a good family and educational background.

Kessai-ken (kase-sie-ken) / This is the authority under which ranking executives approve of a *ringi-sho* proposal, thereby permitting their subordinates to take whatever action the document calls for. Approving a *ringi-sho* [business plan] does not mean, however, that the ranking executive is responsible for the results of the policy or project if it fails. Responsibility falls on all of the managers who stamped the proposal.

Kiboh-taishoku (kee-boh-tie-show-kuu) / This is "compulsory retirement," a system that exists in most Japanese companies practicing lifelong employment. The compulsory retirement age ranges from fifty-five to sixty for most employees. Interestingly enough, *kibo* means "with hope" with the obvious connotation being that retirees hope they will survive to enjoy their retirement. Employees who retire receive a lump sum of money based on their length of service and basic wage. Those employees who retire before reaching the official retirement age receive considerably less in retirement benefits.

Kimochi no shirushi (kee-moe-chee no she-rue-she) / *Kimochi* means "feeling" and *shirushi* means "sign" or "evidence." Put together, they refer to the small gifts Japanese businessmen and others carry with them on trips abroad to give to people who befriend them. Executives making long trips abroad and calling on lots of people may carry three or four dozen *kimochi no shirushi* in their luggage. Foreign businesspeople visiting Japan are not automatically expected to follow the same custom, but it is advisable since it demonstrates both an awareness of Japanese customs and sincerity in establishing the right kind of ties with your Japanese counterparts.

Kimon (kee-moan) / This word originally meant "devil gate" and referred to a gate or door on the northeast corner of a home or building (through which devils were likely to enter, since devils were believed to come from the northeast). Now it is used in reference to a person who is hard to get along with, in the sense of one's personal nemesis. It is used in business when people find they cannot get along with a member of another group or someone in another company. People may say, "They are my *kimon*. Have somebody else go see them." A *kimon* may also be a thing that causes you a lot of trouble, like keeping track of your traveling expenses.

Kone (koe-nay) / This is short for "connections" or "personal connections" through family or school ties. It is a very important asset in Japan's business world.

Konjo (kone-joe) / If foreign businesspeople in Japan want to hire a Japanese salesperson or manager, they should find out if the prospect has *konjo,* which means "fighting spirit." By the same token, foreigners who are negotiating with the Japanese have their work cut out for them if their Japanese counterpart is a *konjo ga aru otoko* (person with fighting spirit). Such people are noted for never letting adversity get them down and never giving up no matter what the odds. In fact, the more resistance they meet, the harder they fight.

Kubi (kuu-bee) / In a country where decapitation by sword was a common form of punishment for many centuries, reference to one's neck was especially meaningful. The term is still used in many key expressions. Some of them: *kubi wo kakete,* stake my neck; *kubi wo kiru,* to cut the neck or fire someone; *kubi wo tobu,* the neck/head flies off, also refers to letting someone go; *kubi ga mawaranai,* neck/head will not turn, said when a person or company is in debt and cannot do much about it; *mawata kubi wo shimeru,* literally to strangle someone with a silken thread or to make conditions so difficult for people that they will leave a company on their own.

Kuromaku (kuu-roe-mah-kuu) / In politics as well as in many industries in Japan, there are usually one or more *kurommaku* or very influential people who have no official office but who exercise decisive power and control most important events. It is often necessary to get the approval and cooperation of these people in political and business situations. The term *kuromaku* means' 'black curtain" and comes from the theater (where it hid those pulling the strings of puppets).

Mae-daoshi (my-dah-oh-she) / Literally "front-loading" (and referring to standing passengers falling forward when the conductor of a subway or train suddenly brakes), *mae-daoshi* is used in a business context to refer to advancing the schedule of a project. The inference is that everyone must make a special effort to move forward together in order for the project to succeed.

Mae muki ni kangaete okimasu (My muu-kee nee khan-guy-ehtay oh-kee-mahss) / *Mae muki ni* means "in the forward direction" and, when preceding *kangaete okimasu,* it means something like "I will give it (your proposition) some thought with the (slight) possibility of moving forward on it." (See *Kangaete okimasu.*)

Mago-koro (mah-go-koe-roe) / This is translated as "true heart" or "sincerity," and is a very important factor in all relations in Japan. Businesspeople in particular expect all of their suppliers and customers to conduct themselves with honesty and integrity, and they are concerned about starting any business with a new company until they are satisfied that their counterparts in the company can be trusted to behave with sincerity and' 'true heart."

Meibutsu (may-ee-boot-sue) / "Famous product." Practically every region or prefecture in Japan has been noted for centuries for one or more of its distinctive products. Always popular with travelers, some of these *meibutsu* are now distributed nationally. There also stores that sell only *meibutsu*. Also, *meibutsu otoko* means "outstanding man."

Meiwaku (may-ee-wah-kuu) / This word means "annoyance" or "trouble." People who cause *meiwaku* in Japan usually get punished one way or another. The word is frequently used in making apologies, i.e. "I didn't mean to cause trouble." In Japan the formal apology generally includes humbling oneself, accepting responsibility, and often making restitution in the form of cash payments for damages, mental suffering, or sickness.

Mekura-ban (may-kuu-rah-bahn) / By itself, *mekura* means "blind." *Ban* means "watchman" or "guard." In combination they refer to executives stamping their name-seal *(hanko)* on a *ringisho* without reading it.

Miso (me-soe) / A salty paste made from soybeans, *miso* is one of the two primary food flavorings (the other is soybean sauce) of Japanese cuisine and represents the essence of the Japanese taste. In business, the term is used either to mean a good or advantageous point or to refer to a blunder of some kind. A product without *miso* has no good points; a product with *miso* has something special about it that makes it easier to sell. Businesses without *miso* are in for a hard time. However, to put *miso* on something, negotiations or whatever, is not a good thing to do it because it makes them look messy and harder to deal with.

Myaku (me-yah-ku) / This is an important word in Japan's business lexicon because it means the "pulse beat" and is used in reference to many areas of business, such as how a presentation is going, how a project is going or in the sense that it is a barometer of business. Japanese businesspeople "read the pulse" of a business project by accumulating and analyzing bits of information from as many sources as possible—a process that can be long and tedious to a foreign contact.

Naikei (nie-kay-ee) / "Unwritten rules," usually referring to various practices followed by lower ranking bureaucrats in the Ministry of Trade and Industry and the Finance Ministry, which often go beyond the laws the ministries are supposed to enforce. These bureaucrats see themselves as Japan's last line of defense against encroachments by foreign businesses into the country.

Najimi (nah-jee-me) / Japanese businesspeople make a special point of meeting and developing friendly relations with managers of restaurants and clubs (and club hostesses) where they go for their own enjoyment as well as for entertaining customers. The aim is to make sure they get good treatment and are not overcharged. A frequent restaurant or cabaret patron is known as an *O-najimi*. If you are the *najimi* of a cabaret hostess, you are a good and favored customer. Having *najimi* in bars and restaurants around town gives you "face." In retail shops, department stores, and other kinds of businesses, a good customer is known as *tokui* (toe-kuu-e) and always gets special attention.

Nakama (nah-kah-mah) / *Nakama* may mean either "companion" or "group," and it is symbolic of the close personal relationship that must exist among Japanese employees for them to function effectively. The term includes connotations of cooperation, conformity, and similarity in thought and behavior, along with the kinds of ties that bind soul mates.

Nakatta koto ni suru (nah-kaht-tah koe-toe nee sue-rue) / This is a term that is often used in Japan in both personal and business situations. It figuratively means "wiping the slate clean" as far as a promise or commitment is concerned—to proceed as if the commitment were not made in the first place. In the case of business where a signed contract is concerned, a penalty may be paid. Even when a penalty is paid and there is agreement between the two parties that it is over, it does not always relieve the paying party from further obligation. The Japanese often ask for a *nakatta koto ni suru* when a situation becomes untenable.

Naruhodo (nah-rue-hoe-doe) / In ordinary conversation between people on the same social or professional level this is a simple word meaning "Is that right! I now (finally) understand. I see. Indeed"—and more or less gives the impression that you agree with whatever the person is saying. It is regarded as impolite for juniors to use the term to seniors. In business, the term is used in the ordinary way, as well as in a formal way, to end discussions or negotiations when one party does not want to make a commitment and does not want to continue the meeting. In this case, it is usually expressed as *"Naruhodo. Yoku wakarimashita. Yoku kento shite mimasu"* ("I see. I understand the matter very well and will give it serious study"). Foreign executives who continue to talk and push after the Japanese use this phrase are not only wasting everyone's time; they may seriously damage their case.

Nawabari (nah-wah-bah-ree) / An old term that referred to a maze of roped-off paths leading into a feudal castle, this term is now used in the sense of "home ground" or "territory" when office workers go out at night to drink at several bars *(hashigo-nomi), i.e.* "ladder drinking." One of the members of the party may say, "This is my *nawabari* (a bar that he frequents often), so everything is on me." It is a way of gaining and keeping "'face" at the bar and obligating friends.

Nenkin seido (nane-keen say-ee-doe) / "Pension system," something that is of vital importance to Japanese workers.

Newaza-shi (nay-wah-zah-she) / A *newaza-shi* is a person who is especially clever at behind-the-scene negotiations and has built up a reputation for being able to do the impossible, usually by pulling some kind of surprise out of the bag. The term comes from the world of judo, where it refers to lying on the mat without moving and suddenly executing an attack *(newaza)* from that position.

Nigiri tsubusu (nee-ghee-ree t'sue-buu-suu) / This literally means' 'to crush by hand," and it refers to managers pigeon-holing a written proposal passed to them by a subordinate. When this happens, junior employees either forget the proposal or take a big chance and go over their boss's head with *a jiki-so* or "direct appeal." In the old days, when underlings went over the head of their feudal lord, they often forfeited their life and sometimes the lives of their families as well. In Japan's business world today people who resort to a *jiki-so* might jeopardize their whole careers if they do not have the support of other strong managers in the company. At the same time, *if the jiki-so* turns out to be accepted by higher-level management the person who crushed it may be the loser.

Nippachi (neep-pah-chee) / Actually this is two words, *ni* (two) and *hachi* (eight), referring to February and August. When combined, the two words are pronounced as *nippachi* and refer to the fact that business is usually at its slowest and lowest in February and August. Because of this, many companies encourage their employees to take their vacations in August. Some companies close down for a week or so during August. A negative aspect of *nippachi* is that businesspeople often use it as an excuse to put off commitments or paying bills for an additional month.

Nuke gake (nuu-kay gah-kay) / Another old term that originally referred to warriors who would steal away from their camp and rush out to meet the enemy first, killing as many as possible in a surprise raid in order to gain respect and receive praise. *Nuke gake* is now used in business in reference to people who attempt to "steal a march" on their colleagues and achieve some kind of major coup before anyone else in the company knows what they are doing. The rare people who succeed in such a *nuke gake* may receive high praise from some of their superiors, but inevitably they are criticized by their colleagues and may endanger their relations with them for the rest of their working lives.

Oitsuke! Oikose! (oh-e-t'sue-kay! oh-e-koe-say!) / When Japan opened its doors to the West in 1854, a slogan that soon became popular was "Oitsuke! Oikose!" which means "Catch up with the West! Pass the West!" The Japanese took the slogan very seriously—and did just that in the 1970s.

O'mono (oh-moe-no) / Literally a "big thing," *O'mono* means an outstanding leader or big shot who is a boss but does not manage directly; people who command such respect that their wishes are carried out without their giving orders. *O'mono* are highly regarded in Japan, and there are always a number of them in business, politics, and in other professions. The *O'mono* are very wise but may often appear simple and even foolish in order not to appear arrogant to their employees or followers. True *O'mono* delegate authority but always take full responsibility for the actions of their underlings.

Onjin (own-jeen) / Literally "obligation person," this refers to a person who helps another in some important area such as getting into a choice school or company. The *onjin* is thereafter "responsible" for the person helped and may act as a go-between in matters relating to them. The person receiving the help is also obligated to the *onjin* for life.

O'rei (oh-ray-ee) / This refers to the etiquette that requires all debts and favors be acknowledged and paid for by bowing, expressing thanks and giving gifts. It is a vital part of social responsibility in Japan.

Otoko ga tatanai (oh-toe-koe gah tah-tah-nie) / "My manhood won't stand up!" This is a phrase that may be used by a man (usually young) when pleading that he be allowed to assume a certain responsibility or be given a certain task for the sake of his "manly honor."

Rikutsu-poi (ree-kute-sue-poy) / *Rikutsu* means "logical" or "reasonable"; *poi* means "in excess" or "to have too much of." A person who is *rikutsu-poi* is too logical, too reasonable; not human enough; ignores the emotional side of things. The Japanese consider most foreigners, especially Americans, as *rikutsu-poi* and therefore difficult or impossible to get along with. Since Americans in particular pride themselves on being logical and reasonable, there is often a fundamental conflict when Japanese and Americans meet. When American executives negotiating with the Japanese run into resistance their natural tendency is to try to carry the day with pure logic and reasonableness. They are often surprised and upset when it doesn't go over.

Saji wo nageru (sah-jee oh nah-gay-rue) / In Japan, people do not "throw in the towel" they "throw in the spoon"—which is what many foreign businesspeople do when they come up against the negotiating and business techniques employed by the Japanese.

Sasen (sah-sen) / *Sasen* literally means "lowering the seating order," which harks back to Japan's feudal period when social and political position was often indicated by where the individual was seated when in attendance on his feudal lord, the Shogun, or members of the Imperial family. Today it is said to be one of the most feared words in the vocabulary of Japanese managers because it refers to being demoted, either by being put into a situation where they have fewer people or no one at all working under them, or by being transferred from the parent company to a subsidiary without being promoted to a higher rank.

Seijitsu (say-ee-jeet-sue) / *Seijitsu* means "sincerity" with a Japanese flavor, of course, meaning that the word has a much broader and deeper use in Japan than elsewhere. The Japanese regard sincerity as the foundation of trust and trust as the foundation for all business dealings—again within the cultural context of Japan. Americans, for example, will do business with the devil if they are offered a good product or a good price. The Japanese give sincerity and trust precedence over product or price and will refuse to do business with companies whose management does not pass their sincerity/trust test.

Senjitsu wa domo arigato gozaimasu (sane-jeet-sue wah doe-moe ah-ree-gah-toe go-zie-mahss) / This is another institutionalized phrase, ritualistically repeated, that plays a key role in Japanese manners and ethics. It means' 'Thank you for the other day," and is said the next time you meet your benefactor after you have been treated to a dinner, lunch, and/or a night on the town. By repeating this phrase, you acknowledge that you are indebted to your host for the hospitality and expect to reciprocate in the future (not necessarily in the same way). If any business understanding was achieved during the eating or drinking bout, this is also the standard phrase to express gratitude.

Sensei (sane-say-ee) / This is the word for "teacher" and is used to address teachers and other professionals, such as lawyers as well as individuals who are highly accomplished in some field. When used in the usual way, it is a term of respect, but it may also be used behind someone's back in a derogatory sense or to his or her face as a bit of flattery or even a friendly insult. The Japanese will frequently address foreigners as *sensei* as a sign of respect. Some also use it as a way of flattering and softening up foreigners who are not familiar with the various uses and nuances of the word.

Sente wo utsu (sane-tay oh uut-sue) / Derived from the Japanese game of *Go,* which is similar to chess and very popular with executives, this phrase means to make a move that forces opponents into an untenable position where they have to move in your favor. It has the connotation of being ahead of the game and is used in reference to business negotiations and other situations.

Senyu koraku (sen-yuu koe-rah-kuu) / Literally "Struggle first; enjoy later," this is a slogan that emphasizes the traditional work ethic of Japanese. It is still a valid factor in Japan's economy, particularly in the number of hours many Japanese work without being paid overtime, and the fact that a significant percentage of the workers, especially on the managerial level, do not take all of the annual holidays they have coming.

Sha-fu (shah-fuu) / *Shafu* are the unwritten rules or codes of a company that apply to the conduct of employees, how they dress and behave to customers and the public, and the image they present. It is also the corporate image of a company—how it is seen in the public eye; as conservative, innovative, progressive, and so on. Japanese companies are very sensitive about their *shafu* and take great pains to mold new employees in the desired image. Once a company's image is damaged, by a scandal or for some other reason, it is very difficult to regain.

Shakun (shah-koon) / *Sha* means "company" and *kun* means "precepts." *Shakun* is the statement of a company's basic philosophy or the company "commandments." A similar word, *shaze* [shah-zay], more or less means "what is right for the company," and it is usually a statement of ideals or principles that is expressed in the form of a motto. Many companies have both *shakun* and *shaze*.

Sha-nai (shah-nie) / This literally means "inside the company" and refers to the many activities within a Japanese company that are regarded as exclusive, private, confidential, or for employees only. Each Japanese company is like an independent society, a community within itself, and things that are described as or labeled as *sha-nai* have more meaning than in the typical Western company. Among the *sha-nai* things in virtually all Japanese companies are *sha-nai ryoko,* company trips; *sha-nai* *kekkon,* company weddings; and *sha-nai yokin,* in-company savings.

Shintai ukagai (sheen-tie uu-kah-guy) / When people in a Japanese company make a costly error or behave in such a way that the company's reputation is harmed, they will often submit a *shintai ukagai,* or "informal resignation," acknowledging responsibility for the wrongdoing, expressing regret, and offering to resign. In the event that they refuse for some reason to submit such a resignation on their own, their superiors or colleagues may urge them to do so, knowing that if they voluntarily take the step, company directors will be much more lenient and possibly let them off with only a token reprimand or minor punishment. In Japan an apology and expression of regret for misbehavior or a crime goes a long way toward expiating guilt. On the other hand, if someone is guilty of breaking the law or company rules and refuses to acknowledge responsibility or express regret, punishment can be severe.

Shiri (she-ree) / The word means "butt," "rear end," "hips," or" ass," depending on the speaker's intent and tone of voice; and it is one of the most useful terms in the language. If people are lazy or slow, they are *shiri ga omoi* (heavy assed). If they really hustle, they *shiri ni hi ga tsuite imasu* (their butt is on fire). If you have to cover up for incompetent colleagues or *shiri nugui,* you' 'wipe their butt. "

Shita-uke (she-tah uu-kay) / A "subcontract firm," a company that depends on other firms, usually larger, for part or all of its business. Most name Japanese manufacturing companies use dozens to hundreds of *shita-uke,* many of which may be operated by former employees, a system that dates back centuries in Japan.

Shonen kyu (show-nane que) / The starting salary for new employees, it literally means "first-year income," which varies according to the size of the company or the educational level.

Shuchu-gou (shuu-chuu-go-uh) / This is a peculiar word that means "downpour" or "torrent-like" as in a severe rainstorm. In the 1960s it was sometimes applied to Japan's style of exporting, meaning that Japanese exporters often totally flooded a market with a particular product, virtually drowning all competition. By the late 1990s China was doing exactly the same thing to the rest of the world, including Japan.

Shukko shain (shuke-koe shah-een) / *Shukko* means "to be on loan" and *sha* means "worker" or "employee"; so a *shukko shain* is one who is on loan to a subsidiary company or affiliated company. The word suggests that the employee will return to the parent or loaning company, but it often happens that the transfer is permanent, particularly when the parent company wants to get rid of the employee concerned. In most cases, employees on loan are selected because the subsidiary or connected company needs help in some specialized area. Since many Japanese companies still do not normally hire from the outside, someone from the parent company is dispatched to help them. It is common for banks to send *shukko shain* to companies that have huge loans outstanding and are having financial difficulties. The *shukko shain* system helps to bind parent and subsidiary companies as well as affiliated or aligned companies together and is thus a part of the "business web" in Japan.

Shumu kisoku (shuu-mu kee-soe-kuu) / These are "rules of employment," something some Japanese workers have to read and sign when they are first hired. Employees of smaller companies are generally more interested in such rules than those who go to work for major corporations, feeling that they need the legal protection provided by the rules.

Shunto (shune-toe) / In 1955, Japan's major union federations devised a cooperative approach to helping workers in different industries gain annual wage increases. This new approach was labeled *Shunto*, which means "Spring Struggle." Several months prior to the annual *base-up* spring wage drive labor leaders meet and decide on demands and possible strike tactics. Generally the unions have reached a consensus by January and their coordinating committee announces the objectives of the forthcoming *Shunto*. Both management and unions are acutely aware of the damage caused by strikes and usually come to an agreement before the "Spring Struggle" occurs. When it is decided to strike, sometimes just as a show of force, the strikes are carefully orchestrated to last only an hour or so and are scheduled so that they cause as little disturbance as possible. For the last several decades the average Japanese worker has missed less than sixteen minutes of work per year as a result of strikes. The only unions in Japan that have staged prolonged strikes, for a week or longer, are generally those representing public workers.

Sobetsu kai (soe-bate-sue kie) / The *sobetsu kai* is a "farewell party," a very popular and common function in japan, held when company employees are assigned overseas or to distant parts of the country, when someone is transferred from one department to another or when someone retires. Sometimes farewell parties and welcome parties for new staff members, returning staff members, or replacements *(kangei kai)* are combined, in which case they are known as *kansogei kai*.

Soko wo nantoku (soe-koe oh nahn-toe-kuu) / If Japanese executives get a pained expression on their face and say, "Soko wo nantoku . . . they are asking you to bend a little or give a little on a particular point because they feel they have gone as far as they can and are giving a sign that they may not be able to accept the deal unless you do. If they add *magete* (mah-gay-tay) or "bend" to the phrase *("Soko wo magete nantoka . . . ")*, the appeal is much stronger.

Soroban to awanai (so-roe-bahn toe ah-wah-nie) / Literally, "It doesn't agree with the abacus," this is an old term used to mean that the price is too high or that a business proposition would not be profitable. It is still used fairly often in informal, casual situations by older people.

Taigu (tie-guu) / This word refers to exceptionally good treatment, service, or entertainment of the kind that is usually provided for people of high rank. A sumptuous dinner may be described as *taigu*. The word also appears on the name cards of individuals to indicate that they have the rank of department or division manager (or some other title) as far as salary and status are concerned, but no employees under them. The *taigu* title was devised to allow people with seniority to be promoted to higher ranks, even though there is no section or department for them to head.

Tamamushi (tah-mah-muu-she) / This is an insect that changes its color to fit its environment. A *tamamushi* contract or decision is one that changes with the viewpoint of the individuals involved. The contract or decision is worded in such a manner that it can be interpreted several different ways, and then the two sides adjust their behavior as they go along in order to make it work. It is a very Japanese thing.

Tana ni ageru (tah-nah nee ah-gay-rue) / The Japanese are reluctant to say "no" outright, and they use a variety of subterfuges to avoid refusing and upsetting someone. One technique is to accept a proposal and then *tana ni ageru* (put it on the shelf). A shorter version of this, *tana-age,* is used when delaying a response or ignoring a matter entirely.

Tanshin funin-sha (tahn-sheen fuu-neen-shah) / This term literally means "one sent alone to a new assignment" and refers to the hundreds of thousands of Japanese men who each year are transferred by their parent companies to branches or subsidiaries in other parts of the country, without their families. These men are known in popular parlance as "business bachelors," and are both the brunt of jokes and the objects of a great deal of sympathy because of the hardships and inconvenience they must often endure, particularly those who are married. A few years ago a man who had been moved 10 times by his company (Mitsubishi Trust & Banking Corporation) published a pamphlet titled *A Guidebook for Tanshin Funin-sha,* which was distributed free to his fellow workers. One of the bits of advice in the booklet was, "Buy at least 20 sets of underwear."

Tarai-mawashi (tah-rie-mah-wah-she) / This is the proverbial "runaround," which is especially popular in Japan, particularly in government offices but also in business and other areas of life. The term *tarai-mawashi* refers to the old stunt of lying on one's back and twirling a wooden washtub with the feet. When you go to government offices, especially to lodge a complaint, you are often sent from one section to another because no one wants to take responsibility for accepting or acting on your complaint. Foreigners visiting Japanese companies without prior

arrangement may feel like they are the victims of *tarai-mawashi* because they do not know which department to go to initially and are frequently shuffled around.

Tataki dai (tah-tah-kee die) / *Tataki dai* literally means "a platform for pounding." It is used in business contexts to mean a suggestion or plan proposed by a lower ranking manager as a starting point for group discussions by all company executives concerned. If a consensus is reached, the plan may be adopted, the equivalent, you might say, of a verbal *ringi-sho*.

Teiki-saiyo (tay-ee-kee-sie-yoe) / In April of each year, larger Japanese companies hire dozens to hundreds of new employees fresh out of high school and college in a system known as *teiki-saiyo,* or "periodic hiring." The bigger corporations do not hire for specific jobs but base the number of new recruits they take in each year on the natural attrition of their whole workforce, growth rate, and long-term strategic planning. The companies usually start the process in the fall of the previous year by inviting seniors in for unofficial interviews (see *aota-gai).* They are bound by an agreement not to start the screening or hiring process before October, but unofficially many of the more desirable students have jobs shortly after the beginning of the senior year. Examinations for company employment are held shortly after the first of each year. After entering their new company, the recruits are put through various training programs, including in some cases training retreats that are similar to military boot camps, where the training is not only intellectual and emotional but also physical.

Tei shisei (tay she-say) / When things go wrong or when someone does not want to get involved or respond, it is common for them to *tei shisei,* or assume a "low posture," "lay low," "keep quiet," hoping that whatever it is will go away. It is as common in business as in private life, and it usually becomes apparent rather quickly.

Tonosama shobai (toe-no-sah-mah show-buy) / In feudal Japan the *tonosama* were clan lords [*daimyo / die-m'yoh, literally "big names"*] who did not engage in business *(shobai)* but still had to deal with merchants in order to manage their fiefs, which basically were self-supporting domains. Having no experience in commercial affairs, and generally being arrogant and presumptuous because of their superior and privileged social rank, the *tonosama* were no match for the quick-witted merchants of Osaka, Nagoya, Edo (Tokyo), and other commercial centers in Japan. Today, companies that made it big in earlier times and make no serious effort to develop new products or to compete as vigorously as new companies that are still struggling to grow are often referred to as doing *tonosama shobai*. Large foreign companies that enter Japan and expect their size and the reputation they have in their own country to sustain them may also be accused of acting like *tonosama*. The accepted Japanese way is for all companies to don the apron of the traditional apprentice *(maedare / my-dah-ray)*; assume a low, humble profile; and work diligently with a true, honest heart.

Tsugo ga warui-no de (t'sue-go gah wah-rue-e-no day) / "Because of an inconvenience"—this is the most common excuse given for breaking an appointment or declining to go somewhere or do something when the individual can't or doesn't want to for whatever reason. No other explanation is given or expected.

Tsuketodoke (t'sue-kay-toe-doe-kay) / The mid-year and year-end gifts that people give to their superiors and benefactors are known as *tsuketodoke*, which literally means "to deliver a bill," but in this case refers rather subtly to "paying off an obligation." *Tsuketodoke* play a significant role in maintaining business as well as personal relationships in Japan.

Tsumiawase (t'sue-me-ah-wah-say) / This is translated as "company gifts" and refers to the gifts (liquor, fruit, and so on) that companies give to customers and connections in midsummer and at the end of the year to help maintain good working relations. The gifts are designed to smooth over any friction that might have developed during the preceding months and to express goodwill and appreciation. *Awase* by itself means "to adjust" or "to bring together" and in this context means to keep good relations on an even keel.

Tsuru no hitokoe (tsu-rue no ssh-toe-koe-eh) / When a group of Japanese in a company or organization is unable to reach a consensus on a topic or problem, the impasse is often broken by *tsuru no hitokoe* or "one word from a crane"—i.e., the president of the company or some other highly placed individual with authority that is unquestioned. The use of the phrase *tsuru no hitokoe* comes from the fact that when a flock of cranes lands to eat, one always stands guard and lets out a loud squawk if any danger approaches.

Uchi (uu-chee) / The word *uchi* literally means "inside" and is commonly used to mean house or home, but it is also synonymous with "our," "my," and "mine" and is used to draw very sharp distinctions between groups. *Uchi no kaisha,* for example, means "our company" or "my company." *Uchi no* by itself means it (or they) belongs to, is part of, my family or company or school or whatever group. Understanding the connotations and importance of *uchi* is essential to understanding the group orientation and behavior of the Japanese.

Uchi-age (uu-chee-ah-gay) / When the Japanese conclude an agreement following a period of negotiations or complete any project, they hold an *uchi-age* drinking party to celebrate the achievement and to reinforce feelings of camaraderie and cooperativeness. The term *uchi-age* actually means to "shoot off' (fireworks) or launch something such as a rocket, so the connotation is that the parties should be loud and lively.

Uchi-awase (uu-chee-ah-wah-say) / *Uchi-awase* literally means something like "to beat out an agreement" and by extension "to achieve harmony." The term, indispensable in Japan, is used to mean a planning session, and it applies to both business and recreation. Virtually all events, including meetings with foreign executives, are preceded by one or more *uchi-awase* during which the participants plan what they are going to do and how they are going to do it. *Uchi-awase* prior to negotiations with foreign companies may go on for several days or even months and are very detailed.

Uka kosaku (uu-kah-koe-sah-kuu) / To "fix something behind the scenes" is often applicable when one is petitioning the government for something or is negotiating a business deal—a common practice in japan.

Undo-kai (uun-doe-kie) / Company *undo-kai* (athletic meets) are common in Japan and are part of the process of building fellowship and solidarity among employees and their families. Managers participate in the meets along with workers.

Wakarimashita (wah-kah-ree-mah-ssh-tah) / "I understand" or "understood." When a Japanese businessperson or politician says *wakarimashita,* there is often an unstated but implied meaning that while they understood what you said they are not agreeing to anything.

Wah-puro (wah-puu-roe) / This is the Japanization of "word processor" and is Japanese as far as the Japanese are concerned. By the same process, a personal computer is a *paso kon* (pah-so kone) and a microcomputer is a *mai-kon* (my-kone).

Wa-kon! Yo-sai! (Wah-kone! Yoe-sie!) / This is a slogan that became popular in Japan during the Meiji period (1868-1912) when the Japanese first began their efforts to catch up with the West in technology and industry. It means "Japanese spirit! Western learning!"

Yakutoku (yah-kuu-toe-kuu) / These are gifts or other benefits that company employees receive because of their positions in their firms. The *yakutoku* are often from suppliers or others doing business with or wanting to do business with the recipient's company. *Yakutoku* may be in the form of gifts, travel, or entertainment. Such fringe benefits are traditional and are regarded as essential to maintaining good human relations, but if they are overdone, if their value is such that there is obviously an ulterior motive on the part of the giver, they may be regarded as an attempt to unduly influence the individual and be rejected. Knowing what constitutes an acceptable gift or benefit in kind is important. If foreign executives are in doubt, they should seek the advice of an experienced friend or adviser.

Yaku tsuki (yah-kuu t'sue-kee) / Literally "with title," this word refers to a person who has a title and is therefore a manager or executive. It can be used to mean anyone above the *sha-in* (company employee) level.

Yoroshiku (yoe-roe-she-kuu) / One of the most frequently used words in the Japanese language, this means "Please do whatever you can for me/us!" in any situation where you want someone else's cooperation, help, or goodwill. It is used in a multitude of situations, with the meaning varying to fit the circumstance, and is a strong, personal appeal. The full, polite phrase is *Yoroshiku onegaishimasu* (Yoe-roe-she-kuu oh-nay-guy-she-mahss).

Yukitsuke no ba (yuu-kee-skay no bah) / This is "favorite bar," and virtually all Japanese managers have one (or two or more). Establishing a relationship with bar managers, bartenders, and bar or club hostesses is one of the requirements of doing business in Japan, not only to avoid being taken by underworld-connected bars but also to assure good service when one entertains clients or subordinates, to demonstrate' 'face," and to be able to presume upon the goodwill and interest of the bar owner/manager. Favorite bars are part of the individual manager's network.

Yuryokusha (yuu-ree-yoe-kuu-shah) / "A person with influence," or someone who has enough clout or pull to get the son or daughter of a friend or relative a job in a desirable company, or to achieve some other goal or action.

Zaibatsu (zie-baht-sue) / "Financial clique," or a large industrial combine, often monopolistic in practice if not in principle.

Ten or so of Japan's largest *zaibatsu* (Mitsui, Mitsubishi, and C. Itoh, etc.) control over fifty percent of the country's import and export business. In pre-World War II Japan the Mitsui conglomerate had over three million employees.

Zaikai jin (zie-kie jeen) / *Zaikai* means something like "high finance" or "financial circles," and *jin* means" person. "Combined, the word refers to a distinguished, generally wealthy, senior man, often retired from the highest levels of business or finance, who acts as a neutral counselor for major firms or groups involved in important deals. A variation of this term also used in reference to these high-level go-betweens is *zaikai shidosha* (she-doe-shah); *shidosha* means "leader" or "expert."

Zensho shimasu (zen-show she-mahss) / This is a term that frequently misleads and frustrates Western diplomats and politicians as well as business executives. It means "I will do my best," but is also sometimes translated as "I will take care of it," which is something altogether different. A Japanese prime minister once used the phrase to an American president, who was pressing him about something, and the U.S. president went back to Washington, D. C., believing he had a firm commitment. When the prime minister failed to deliver, the American president was very upset. Executives should keep in mind that the downside of "I will do my best" is "Even though what you ask is impossible, I will do my best."

###

www.ingramcontent.com/pod-product-compliance
Lightning Source LLC
Chambersburg PA
CBHW030938180526
45163CB00002B/611